Old West

SHOWDOWN

Old West

SHOWDOWN

TWO AUTHORS WRANGLE OVER THE TRUTH ABOUT
THE MYTHIC OLD WEST

BILL MARKLEY AND
KELLEN CUTSFORTH

TWODOT®

GUILFORD, CONNECTICUT
HELENA, MONTANA

A · TWODOT® · BOOK

An imprint of Globe Pequot
An imprint and registered trademark of Rowman & Littlefield

Distributed by NATIONAL BOOK NETWORK

British Library Cataloguing in Publication Information available

Library of Congress Cataloging-in-Publication Data Available

ISBN 9781493032167 (cloth : alk. paper)
ISBN 9781493032174 (electronic)

∞™ The paper used in this publication meets the minimum requirements of American National Standard for Information Sciences—Permanence of Paper for Printed Library Materials, ANSI/NISO Z39.48-1992.

Printed in the United States of America

CONTENTS

FOREWORD

Chris Enss

HISTORY IS DEFINED AS THE STUDY OF PAST EVENTS. PAST EVENTS prove, however, that history is more than just what happened when—it's a complex intersection of truths, biases, and hopes. It can be remembered, recovered, or even invented. These facts are why some believe that there were two shooters on the grassy knoll when President John F. Kennedy was killed, that man never walked on the Moon, and that Elvis Presley is not only alive but also serving coffee at an out-of-the-way diner in Tulsa, Oklahoma.

History is a deeply controversial subject. Historical research is not an exact science, and that's one of the reasons why historians often disagree with those who draw definitive conclusions. New information on historical events or figures is uncovered constantly. Those findings cause new conclusions to be drawn. Historians at times debate those conclusions, citing faulty interpretation of the evidence. The role of ideology and politics comes into play when explaining new findings, which accounts for why some believe that George Washington chopped down a cherry tree; that Benjamin Franklin flew a kite with a house key attached to the string during a lightning storm, proving that lightning had an electrical nature; and that Abraham Lincoln had a rare, genetic disorder known as Marfan syndrome and would have died soon enough without John Wilkes Booth's help.

History has its own history. It's made up of multiple accounts and multiple perspectives, which lead to multiple discussions and disagreements. Author and playwright Oscar Wilde once wrote of history, "Nothing that actually happened matters in the slightest." There are numerous historians still debating what occurred at the Battle of the Little Bighorn, who was involved in the Johnson County War, and the circumstances leading up to the night that Billy the Kid was shot and killed. For them, what happened matters a great deal. Authors and historians Bill Markley and Kellen Cutsforth have given voice to those who dispute the findings around ten historical accounts. *Old West Showdown* looks at both sides of controversial events that took place in the Old West and debates the conclusions.

Were Wyatt Earp and Doc Holliday heroes or simply gunslingers out to settle a score? That's just as explosive a question today as it was in October 1881, when the gunfight at the O.K. Corral took place. The passage of time has not made it a safe or dull topic. The same holds true when discussing Wild Bill Hickok's first gunfight or the death of Crazy Horse, which are all topics covered in *Old West Showdown*. Feelings run deep when it comes to these subject matters—so much so that the debate over what actually happened will never be settled.

The great art of being a historian involves an ability to sift through incomplete or conflicting evidence—and to make a case for an overview that unifies what's known. Only by debating and disagreeing can historians improve their theories and the overall quality of their work. *Old West Showdown* helps move that process along.

INTRODUCTION

THE WEST. JUST SAYING THOSE TWO WORDS BRINGS VIVID IMAGES OF the American West to mind for millions of people around the world: images of endless plains, scorching deserts, and icy mountain ranges; images of thundering buffalo herds, coiled rattlesnakes, and roaring grizzly bears; and images of resourceful Indians, hardy pioneers, wily desperados, and determined lawmen.

The story of the settling of the West has been told countless ways by many people. Along the way, some stories have become distorted, sometimes by mistake and sometimes on purpose. Why not stretch the tale a bit just to make it more interesting? Other incidents were controversial right from the start and to this day have strong adherents on each side.

Bill Markley and Kellen Cutsforth have selected ten such Old West stories and characters to explore in this book. These are popular figures and incidents that most people have at least heard of (and may even know a little of the story).

How did the gunfight at the O.K. Corral actually unfold? Did it really happen the way it is presented to us in movie theaters and on television screens? Was it black and white? Were the Earps and Doc Holliday the good guys and the Clantons and McLaurys the bad guys?

Jesse and Frank James and the Younger brothers were notorious outlaws loved by many and hated by others. Why did they leave their well-known haunts in Missouri and travel to Minnesota to rob a bank in Northfield?

Wild Bill Hickok is one of the best-known gunfighters in the Old West, but did his first gunfight, which brought him national renown, happen the way it was reported in the press?

Calamity Jane is probably the best-known woman in the Old West. She became a legend in her own time, and her reputation carries on today. But did she do all the things she claimed she did? Were she and Wild Bill lovers?

And then, of course, there's General George Armstrong Custer's last stand at the Little Bighorn. Today, many believe that his ego led to his demise—or did it? Did the officers under his command let him down?

Buffalo Bill Cody—everyone loves Buffalo Bill, who brought the West to the East with his Wild West. But did he really do all the things he claimed he did, including riding for the Pony Express and killing the Cheyenne leader Tall Bull?

One of the most tragic occurrences on the northern plains was the death of the Lakota leader Crazy Horse. Was his death a random accident, or was his killing arranged by the army to get him out of the way, or was it intertribal politics that got him killed?

Then there's Pat Garrett and Billy the Kid. Garrett claimed that he shot and killed Billy one night at Fort Sumner, but was it a cover-up? Did the Kid get away and live to an old age in Texas?

Geronimo was one of the most feared Apache killers in the American Southwest and Mexico in the late nineteenth century. Today, however, many people see him only as someone fighting for the right to maintain his way of life. Which was it?

The last chapter explores Wyoming's Johnson County War. The large ranchers claimed the small ranchers were nothing more than rustlers, but were they?

Bill Markley and Kellen Cutsforth take opposing points of view on these stories. Each chapter is a stand-alone tale from the Old West, divided into three parts. The first part sets the stage for the story and relates the facts that most historians agree upon. In the second part, one author takes one side of the story, and the third part is the other author taking an opposing view. For instance, in the case of the gunfight at the O.K. Corral, the first part of the chapter sets the scene for the gunfight using information that almost everyone agrees upon. Kellen subsequently takes the Earp and Doc Holliday side of the story, and then Bill tells the Clanton and McLaury side of the story.

Bill and Kellen expect people to disagree with some of the controversial topics covered here as they fan the flames of controversy, but, in so doing, they hope that you, the reader, will rekindle your interest in these stories from our history and conduct your own research to uncover what really is true. It's time to start the showdown.

Chapter One

THE GUNFIGHT AT THE O.K. CORRAL

JUST THE FACTS

ICONIC MOVIES SUCH AS *TOMBSTONE* (1993) AND *THE GUNFIGHT AT THE O.K. Corral* (1957) show three Earp brothers and their trusty sidekick Doc Holliday marching down Tombstone's dusty streets to their rendezvous with destiny. But how did the gunfight really go down? And what were the reasons behind it?

Tombstone, Arizona Territory, boomed into existence after the discovery of silver ore in 1877. In surrounding Cochise County, ranchers provided beef cattle to reservations, military posts, and Tombstone residents. A lawless element of ranchers and rustlers also operated in these rural surroundings and were often referred to as *Cowboys.* Among these Cowboys were two prominent ranching families, the Clantons and McLaurys, who were good friends. Tombstone residents were divided in their loyalties to the Cowboys. If they had business dealings with the Cowboys, those townspeople normally sided with them in any disputes.

Entering this mix came the Earp brothers—Wyatt, Virgil, Morgan, and James—eager to make their fortunes, as well as Wyatt's friend, hot-tempered gambler Doc Holliday. By 1881, Virgil, as a deputy US marshal who later served in dual roles after being appointed Tombstone's marshal, attempted to control the Cowboys, while Cochise County sheriff Johnny Behan supported the Cowboys and was an Earp rival. Relations between the Earps, Clantons, and McLaurys deteriorated into a series of disputes and failed business dealings between the three families, culminating in the Wild West's most famous gunfight.

On October 25, 1881, Ike Clanton and Tom McLaury arrived in Tombstone on business. Ike proceeded to go on an all-night drinking spree. Inebriated, Ike made numerous threats against the Earps and Holliday, and they made threats back. The next morning, Ike began roaming the streets with a Winchester and a six-shooter. Around noon, Virgil disarmed him, and then he hauled Ike to court for violating Tombstone's ordinance banning firearms. Receiving a fine, Ike was released. Following Ike's time before the judge, Wyatt Earp and Tom McLaury threatened each other. Wyatt followed up his threats by slapping Tom's face and striking him with his gun.

Around this time, Billy Clanton and Frank McLaury rode into town to conduct some business. Billy Claiborne, a friend of the Clantons and McLaurys, told Billy Clanton about Ike's confrontations. Worried about the brewing trouble, Billy Clanton tracked down Ike to get him out of town, and the McLaurys determined that they would leave after they settled their business. Preparing to depart, the Clantons and McLaurys gathered near the rear entrance to the O.K. Corral. (A little-known fact: The ensuing gunfight took place in an empty lot on Fremont Street between Fly's Boarding House and a home owned by a man named William Harwood.)

Not knowing that the Cowboys were preparing to leave, Virgil learned the Clantons and McLaurys were carrying guns, and he planned to disarm them, adhering to the city firearms ban. Gathering his deputy brothers Morgan and Wyatt, Virgil also temporarily deputized Doc Holliday and handed him a shotgun. The men proceeded down Fourth Street, then turned left on Fremont toward the Cowboys and destiny. Sheriff Behan, who was ahead of the Earps, attempted to disarm the Cowboys, but they would have none of it. He then tried to stop the Earps, but they shoved him aside, marching on to confront the Cowboys, with Behan trailing close behind.

After coming face to face with the Cowboy contingent in the empty lot, Virgil commanded them to surrender their weapons. History becomes hazy at this point, with each side proclaiming the other fired first. But when bullets started flying, many historians believe the fight happened as follows.

Two shots rang out simultaneously, with Wyatt hitting Frank McLaury in the stomach and the second bullet finding no target. Morgan then fired at Billy Clanton, hitting him in the right wrist and chest. Billy was shot again, this time in the stomach, causing him to slide toward the ground while firing his pistol left-handed. Stepping in, Behan snatched Billy Claiborne and pulled him into Fly's Boarding House. Ike, unarmed, grabbed Wyatt and was told by Wyatt, "Go to fighting or get away." Ike then ran through Fly's front door and out the back. Tom McLaury took cover behind the horse he was holding. Doc drew down on him with the shotgun and blasted him under the right armpit. Mortally wounded, Tom staggered onto Third Street, where he collapsed and later died.

With the cracking of gun-shots, Frank McLaury tried to retrieve his Winchester from its saddle scabbard as his horse started to bolt. As bullets continued to fly, one hit Virgil in the ankle, throwing him to the ground. Seeing his fallen comrade, Doc dropped his shotgun and drew his pistol at the same moment Frank drew his. The two fired at each other, and Morgan discharged his pistol at Frank as well.

Frank was killed in the exchange, but his bullet nicked Doc's hip. Billy Clanton then shot Morgan in the shoulder. In the same instant, Morgan and Wyatt unloaded on Billy, piercing him below the ribs. In about thirty

Wyatt Earp, photo taken in Dodge City, Kansas, 1870s. COURTESY OF DENVER PUBLIC LIBRARY, WESTERN HISTORY COLLECTION (Z-246)

seconds, nearly thirty shots were fired, leaving the McLaury brothers and Billy Clanton dead or dying and Morgan and Virgil Earp and Doc Holliday wounded. Following the gunfight, a running battle continues to this day over what happened that fateful afternoon and over who was responsible for the immense bloodshed.

A Case for the Earps——Kellen Cutsforth

The gunfight at the O.K. Corral was not all that well known until 1931, following the publication of the book *Wyatt Earp: Frontier Marshall* by Stuart Lake. This volume was a best seller and introduced the public to the lawman Wyatt Earp, his sidekick Doc Holliday, and the gunfight at the O.K. Corral. In the years following Lake's publication, thousands of books, articles, and movies have been produced covering the legendary battle and the characters involved.

Authors, historians, and filmmakers often come to different conclusions concerning this landmark moment in the Old West. Some seek to create heroes, some aim to rewrite history, and others simply look to tell the truth. But with a historic event blurred in so much mystery and myth, the unvarnished truth can often be difficult to unearth. In the years following the gunfight, questions have arisen as to the motivations of its participants.

Were the Earps in the right confronting the Clanton and McLaury brothers on that fateful October day? Did they murder defenseless men to settle a grudge? Were the Clantons and McLaurys nothing more than rustlers who got what was coming to them? To answer these questions, it is best to review the accepted facts and leave all other theories behind the saloon's swinging doors.

When the Earp brothers arrived in the silver mining town of Tombstone, Arizona Territory, in 1879, the little burg seemed to be nothing more than a tent colony. Virgil Earp, the oldest of the five Earp brothers, had been recently hired as a deputy US marshal for eastern Pima County, with his offices stationed in Tombstone.[1] Accompanied by his brothers James and Wyatt, and later Morgan, the men found the small tent town home to roughly one hundred residents sprinkled among numerous silver mines.[2] Two years following the Earps' arrival, however, Tombstone "boomed," and the population exploded to well over seven thousand. With this growth came conflict between local rustlers and the town's new business interests.

The rural rustlers were a loose affiliation of men often referred to as *Cowboys*. These bandits made their living by smuggling stolen cattle, horses, tobacco, and alcohol over the Mexican border, about thirty miles away from the Arizona territorial line, and then selling the contraband for a pretty profit. When they weren't rustling livestock, these desperadoes robbed stagecoaches as a separate means of income.[3]

These thefts hurt Tombstone residents relying on the goods carried by the coaches. They also damaged the confidence of investors living in cities like San Francisco, who were betting on the continuing silver boom. The Cowboy criminals were loosely led by brothers Tom and Frank McLaury, brothers Billy and Ike Clanton, "Curly" Bill Brocius, and Johnny Ringo.

Most of the residents of Tombstone did not have high opinions of these men. In fact, George Parson, a diarist and Tombstone resident (whose diary is relied upon as one of the most accurate firsthand accounts of life in Tombstone), wrote of the gang, "A Cowboy is a rustler at times, and a rustler is a synonym for desperado—bandit, outlaw, and horse thief." Along with the Parson diary, a respected business paper, the *San Francisco Daily Exchange*, wrote of the Cowboy scourge, declaring, "The cowboy class are the most despicable beings on the face of the earth. They are a terror to decent people and a disgrace to even frontier civilization." With sentiments like these coming from Tombstone's citizens and people around the country, it is easy to see why the lawmen Earp brothers eventually came into conflict with the Cowboys.

Virgil Earp, as a deputy US marshal, first encountered the Cowboys in the summer of 1880, when he and his brothers Wyatt and Morgan tracked six stolen US Army mules to the McLaury ranch and discovered several Cowboys trying to alter their brands with running irons. After Frank McLaury was charged in the theft, he threatened Virgil's life and soon became an enemy of the Earps.[4]

Animosity percolated between the Earp faction and the Cowboys through several more events leading up to the O.K. Corral gunfight. It truly came to a boil, however, over one incident. On March 15, 1881, four Cowboys held up a Wells Fargo stagecoach on its way through Contention, Arizona Territory, which was carrying $26,000 in silver bullion. During the robbery, the stage driver and an accompanying passenger were murdered.[5]

Following this hijacking, a posse was assembled by Cochise County sheriff Johnny Behan that included Virgil, Wyatt, and Morgan Earp, among others. The posse scoured the countryside for the bandits and captured Cowboy Luther King hiding at a ranch that was sympathetic to the Cowboy gangsters. During interrogation, King divulged that he was in on the robbery and named Cowboys Bill Leonard, Harry "the Kid" Head, and Jim Crane as conspirators.[6] Behan returned to Tombstone with the captured desperado while the Earps continued their search for the rest of the villains.

Behan, who had a reputation for being sympathetic to the Cowboys, inexplicably allowed King to easily escape and ride to freedom. This incident enraged the Earp brothers and motivated Wyatt to seek to replace Behan in the upcoming county sheriff election. At that point, Wyatt hatched a plan to help himself win the election by capturing the murderous stage robbers.

Ike Clanton, who knew the whereabouts of his Cowboy counterparts, struck a deal with Wyatt to help him capture the outlaws. In exchange for his help, Wyatt offered Ike the reward money for the bandits ($1,200 per head), as well as a sum of cash from his own pocket, all totaling $6,000.[7]

Unfortunately for Wyatt, the agreement never came to fruition. Both Leonard and Head were killed by brothers Ike and Billy Haslett, men with whom they had a long-standing quarrel. It is believed that Crane then took retribution for the deaths of his partners and murdered the Haslett brothers. Most inhabitants of Tombstone were frightened by these events because it appeared that the Cowboys were no longer just a guild of thieves but a bloodthirsty, vengeful fighting force willing to take on anyone.[8]

After this episode, Ike Clanton began drinking heavily and accusing Wyatt of blabbing about their secret arrangement. Ike believed that

Wyatt, his brothers, or Doc Holliday would let word slip about the arrangement and that his Cowboy pals would eventually murder him too.[9]

Through most of the summer and into early October 1881, eyewitness accounts described Ike Clanton's behavior as increasingly threatening. He threatened the Earp brothers' lives and riled up his Cowboy compatriots. And Virgil Earp testified that Johnny Ringo even swore a blood oath to kill Virgil and his brothers.[10]

These threats brought Wyatt's good friend and dentist by trade, Doc Holliday, into the feud. Doc stood by the Earps and returned threats against Ike and the McLaurys, saying he would "make a fight if they wanted one."[11] Ike, in turn, accused Doc of knowing about Wyatt and his arrangement and blabbing about it.

In the early morning hours of October 26, Ike Clanton and Doc Holliday quarreled in one of Tombstone's saloons, with Ike shooting his mouth off. The quarrel eventually spilled into the street, forcing deputy marshals Morgan, Virgil, and Wyatt Earp to break up the dispute with threats of jail time for both men.[12]

After their argument ended with no resolution, each man went his own way. Ike headed back into the saloon, where he went on to get very drunk and become quite belligerent. He then proceeded to the Occidental Saloon down the street and joined a poker game whose participants included Tom McLaury, Sheriff Johnny Behan, and Virgil Earp. The men played until the early morning hours that day. Throwing down a winning hand, Virgil drew the ire of both Tom and Ike.

After bowing out of the game, Virgil left for home. Ike, completely drunk, gave a message to him meant for Doc Holliday: "[Tell] that son of a bitch [he] has got to fight." When Virgil responded that he would not deliver the vulgar message, Ike told the oldest Earp brother, "You may have to fight before you know it." Virgil took Ike's ranting as nothing more than the ramblings of an angry drunk and went home.[13]

Ike Clanton's day, however, did not end there. He hopped from saloon to saloon, becoming more inebriated, violent, and boisterous. Ike also began openly carrying firearms in town, which was illegal within the city limits, and he was quoted as having said, "As soon as the Earps and

Doc Holliday showed themselves on the street, the ball would open, and they would have to fight."[14]

After hearing of Ike's warnings, the Earps shrugged them off as the talk of a drunken loudmouth. The bluster and bravado, however, did not sit well with Doc Holliday, who immediately jumped out of bed to confront the Cowboy. When the Earps heard what was brewing, they found Ike stumbling through the dusty streets of Tombstone with a rifle in his hands and a revolver in his belt. Virgil quickly disarmed Ike from behind, taking his rifle and bludgeoning him unconscious.[15]

After heading to the courthouse, Ike was forced to pay a fine for his conduct. At the same time, Wyatt encountered Tom McLaury, who had come to check on his Cowboy comrade. Words were exchanged between the two, ending with Wyatt using his pistol to club Tom about the head.[16] Fearing a gunfight, Cowboys Frank and Tom McLaury, nineteen-year-old Billy Clanton, and their friend Billy Claiborne met at the local gun shop to load up on ammunition and were also joined by Ike as Wyatt Earp watched them through a window.[17] While in the gun store, Ike was not allowed to buy a shooting iron because of his inebriated condition, as well as the threats he had been making all over town.

Much innuendo and gossip traveled from one citizen's mouth to the next through the streets of Tombstone that infamous day, causing the Earps and Holliday to feel certain that they were in for an assassination attempt from the Cowboy contingent. Virgil Earp pleaded with Sheriff Behan to help disarm the Cowboys, but Behan said that if he and Earp showed up together, there would surely be a firefight. So Behan decided that he would disarm the Cowboys himself.[18]

Behan, of course, did not disarm his Cowboy buddies, and their threats continued until the Earps defended themselves by confronting their enemies on Fremont Street. Much of the blame for the bloodletting that day can be heaped upon the head of Ike Clanton. He was a proven rustler who associated with known murderers. He tended to shoot his mouth off when intoxicated and made enemies of the Earps through his own paranoia and distrust.

Ike's delusional fear of his deal with Wyatt being discovered by his cutthroat associates directly led to the Wild West's most famous gun battle and the deaths of his brother and friends. The Earps had every right to fear for their lives, with the murders during the stagecoach robbery and the brutal executions of the Haslett brothers taking place at the hands of the Cowboy gang whose members were now threatening them.

Blame should also fall on Sheriff Johnny Behan, who was nothing more than a shill for the Cowboys and allowed known murderer and Cowboy confidant Luther King to escape justice. He further stirred the animosity between the Cowboys and the Earps that fateful day when he professed to have disarmed the Cowboys when clearly he had not. Who shot first will never be proven and does not matter because it is all speculation. Clearly, the Cowboys were ready for a fight and not defenseless, as evidenced by the injuries sustained by Doc Holliday, Virgil Earp, and Morgan Earp.

Furthermore, Sheriff Behan was in the tank for the Cowboys and, as a result, testified on their behalf during the coroner's inquest. Ike Clanton's testimony during the same inquest reads as the recollections of a rambling drunk, which witnesses on both sides admit he most certainly was. In my opinion, any case made against the Earps is nothing more than revisionist history in a vain attempt to make villains out of victims.

A Case for the Clantons and McLaurys——Bill Markley

The Earps and Doc Holliday never gave the McLaury brothers and nineteen-year-old Billy Clanton a chance, murdering them behind the O.K. Corral.

When Ike Clanton and Tom McLaury arrived in Tombstone on October 25, 1881, they came strictly for business and planned to spend the night. Ike began a drinking spree, making the rounds of the saloons while criticizing the Earps and Holliday.

About one o'clock in the morning on October 26, Ike entered the Alhambra Saloon, sitting down at a table for a meal. Wyatt and Morgan Earp were at the counter when Holliday entered. Seeing Ike, Holliday walked up to his table, cursing him and calling him "a son of a bitch of a cowboy" who "had been using his name." Holliday told Ike to get out his gun and get to work. Ike replied that he didn't have a gun on him. Holliday called him "a damned liar" and said Ike had threatened the Earps. Ike later testified, "I told him I had not [threatened the Earps and] to bring whoever said so to me and I would convince him that I had not. He told me again to pull out my gun and if there is any grit in me, to go to fighting. All the time he was talking . . . he had his hand in his bosom, and I supposed on his pistol. I looked behind me and I saw Morgan Earp. . . . He had his hand in his bosom also, looking at me."

Morgan led the hothead Holliday outside. Ike said of the event:

> *I then got up and went out on the sidewalk. Doc Holliday said, "You son of a bitch, if you ain't heeled, go heel yourself."[19] . . . Morgan then stepped up and said, "Yes, you son-of-a-bitch, you can have all the fight you want now!" I thanked him and told him I did not want any of it now. I was not heeled. Virgil Earp stood off about 10 to 15 feet from us . . . Wyatt Earp came up . . . Wyatt did not say anything. Morgan Earp told me if I was not heeled, when I came back on the street to be heeled. I walked off and asked them not to shoot me in the back.[20]*

Soon after these events, Ike entered the Occidental Saloon, joining an all-night poker game with Virgil Earp, Tom McLaury, and Sheriff Johnny Behan. After Morgan had earlier warned him to arm himself, Ike got his Winchester and pistol, and then he continued his saloon drinking tour, badmouthing the Earps. Around noon, Virgil and Morgan came up behind Ike. Virgil struck him on the side of the head with a six-shooter, knocking him against a wall. Ike testified, "Morgan Earp cocked his pistol and stuck it at me. Virgil Earp took my six shooter and Winchester. . . . They pulled me along and said, 'You damned son of a bitch, we'll take you up here to Judge Wallace's.'"[21]

Dragging Ike to the Recorder's Office, Virgil searched for Judge Wallace while Morgan guarded Ike. Wyatt arrived, saying to Ike, "You damn dirty cow thief, you have been threatening our lives, and I know it. I think I would be justified to shooting you down any place I would meet you, but if you are anxious to make a fight, I will go anywhere on earth to make a fight with you, even over to San Simon, among your crowd." Fed up with the threats, Ike responded by saying, "Fight is my racket and all I want is four feet of ground."[22]

Morgan and Ike argued about his arrest.[23] Morgan offered to pay Ike's fine if Ike would fight. "I'll fight you anywhere or any way," Ike replied. Morgan offered a weapon, but Ike declined, saying that he did not like the odds. After the exchange of threats, Judge Wallace arrived, fined Ike for carrying firearms in town, and released him.[24]

At this point, Tom McLaury arrived on the street in front of the courtroom to check on Ike. Seeing Tom, Wyatt asked him, "Are you heeled?" Tom replied that he had never done anything against the

Doc Holliday, dentist and gambler by trade and good friend of Wyatt Earp.
COURTESY OF DENVER PUBLIC LIBRARY, WESTERN HISTORY COLLECTION (Z-8850)

Earps and that he was Wyatt's friend. But Tom went on to say, "If you want to make a fight, I'll make a fight with you anywhere." "All right, make a fight," Wyatt said, slapping Tom's face with his left hand, then striking the side of Tom's head with his pistol in his right hand, bloodying Tom's face.[25]

"I could kill the son-of-a-bitch," Apolinar Bauer, a Tombstone resident, testified that Wyatt had said after hitting Tom "two, three, maybe four" times with his pistol. Lying in the street, Tom "opened his eyes up large and trembled all over."[26]

Billy Clanton and Frank McLaury rode into town, stopping at the Grand Hotel. "How are you?" Doc Holliday greeted them and shook hands in passing. As they ordered drinks, Billy Allen, another Tombstone resident, walked in and told Frank that Wyatt had pistol-whipped Tom. "What did he hit Tom for?" Frank asked. Allen said he didn't know, and Frank responded by saying, "I will get the boys out of town. We won't drink." He and Billy Clanton left without touching their drinks and rode west on Allen Street toward the O.K. Corral.[27]

On their way, they ran into Billy Claiborne, who had taken Ike to the doctor. He told them what had happened to Ike. "Billy asked me where was Ike," Claiborne later testified. "[Billy Clanton said,] 'I want to get him to go out home.' He said he did not come here to fight anyone, 'and no one didn't want to fight me.'"[28] They met Tom and Ike at Spangenberg's Gun Shop. Frank and Billy bought ammunition and Ike wanted to buy a pistol, but owner George Spangenberg would not sell him one. They left, heading west on Allen Street to Dexter's Livery and Feed Stables, and then crossed Allen Street to the O.K. Corral. The two Billys walked through the corral to the vacant lot on Fremont Street where Ike was having his team harnessed;[29] Ike joined them while the McLaurys went through the corral's rear entrance to Bauer's Union Meat Market on Fremont Street.

About 1:30 p.m., Sheriff Behan was getting a shave at Barron's Barbershop when someone said that "there was liable to be trouble between the Earps and Clantons." This was the first Behan had heard that there were problems. He found Virgil at Hafford's Corner Saloon and asked what was going on. Virgil responded that there was "a lot of sons of bitches in town looking for a fight." Behan replied, "You had better disarm the crowd." Virgil said he would not; he would give them a chance to fight. Behan said, "It is your duty as a peace officer instead of encouraging a fight to disarm the parties."[30] Behan then left to disarm the Cowboys.

Learning that the Cowboys were on Fremont Street, Virgil decided to go disarm them himself, taking along Wyatt, Morgan, and a temporarily deputized Doc Holliday. He gave Holliday his shotgun, which Holliday concealed under his long coat.

Behan found Frank McLaury outside Bauer's Union Meat Market and told him to give up his weapon. Frank replied he did not intend to cause any trouble but that he would only give up his guns after Behan had disarmed the Earps.[31]

Behan walked with Frank, leading his horse westward to the vacant lot where Tom, Billy Claiborne, and the Clantons stood. The sheriff searched Ike, finding no weapons. Tom opened his coat, saying he carried no guns. Seeing the Earps and Holliday approaching, Behan told the Cowboys, "Wait here. I see them coming down. I will go up and stop them."[32] As Behan walked toward the Earps, Ruben Coleman, an eyewitness, heard one of the Clantons say, "You need not be afraid Johnny, we are not going to have any trouble."[33]

Martha King was in Bauer's Union Meat Market when someone at the door said, "There they come." She stepped to the door and saw Holliday and the Earps pass on the sidewalk. She testified, "What frightened me and made me run back, [is] I heard this man [one of the Earps] on the outside, looked at Holliday, and I heard him say 'Let them have it,' and Doc Holliday said, 'All right.'"[34]

Behan testified that he intercepted the Earps and Holliday: "I told them not to go any further, that I was down there for the purpose of disarming the Clantons and McLaurys." They ignored him, but he continued talking: "Gentlemen, I am sheriff of this county, and I am not going to allow any trouble if I can help it." They brushed past, but he followed, calling for them to stop.[35] Virgil said, "Johnny, I am going to disarm them."[36]

The Cowboys stood talking with the horses saddled in the vacant lot and their backs to the Harwood house. The Earps and Holliday stopped about six feet from them.[37] Behan and Billy Claiborne both moved toward the front door of Fly's Boarding House.

Behan saw that the Earps and Holliday had drawn their pistols. A nickel-plated pistol was pointed at Billy Clanton, which Behan thought Holliday was holding. An Earp, possibly Wyatt, said, "You sons of bitches, you have been looking for a fight, and now you can have it!" Virgil yelled, "Boys, throw up your hands, I want your guns." Billy Clanton responded, saying, "Don't shoot me. I don't want to fight!" and Tom McLaury threw open his coat, saying, "I'm not armed," as the Earp party opened fire.[38]

Billy Allen had followed behind the Earps and saw Holliday fire the first shot and an Earp fire the second.[39] Behan testified that the first shot was fired from the nickel-plated pistol, followed immediately by a second shot from a different Earp pistol.[40] Holliday's weapon of choice was a .38 caliber nickel-plated 1877 Colt Lightning.[41] There was a pause, and then Behan thought the next eight to ten shots were from the Earp party.[42]

Gambler Wesley Fuller saw Billy Clanton throw up his hands, saying, "Don't shoot me! I don't want to fight!" and Frank held his horse with no weapons in his hands. Ike and Tom were not armed. Holliday and Morgan Earp fired the first two shots. The Earps and Holliday got off six or seven shots before Billy Clanton and Frank McLaury could draw their pistols.[43]

Billy Claiborne said the Clantons held their hands in the air and Tom opened his coat, saying, "I haven't got anything boys, I'm disarmed!" Holliday fired first, hitting Tom, and Morgan fired second, hitting Billy Clanton, who slid to the ground. "Billy Clanton drew his six-shooter and threw across his leg as he lay on the ground and commenced shooting."[44]

Ike later testified that he was getting ready to leave town when the Earps arrived and that the Cowboys had their hands in the air when Holliday and Morgan fired the first shots. The follow-up shots all came from the Earp side. Unarmed, Ike stood in front of Wyatt. "He shoved his pistol against my belly, and told me to throw up my hands. He said, 'You son of a bitch, you can have a fight.' I . . . [took] Wyatt Earp's hand and pistol with my left hand and grabbed him around the shoulder with my right hand and held him for a few seconds. While I was holding him, he shot." Ike pushed Wyatt away and ran through the front door of Fly's Boarding House and out the back.[45]

After thirty shots in half a minute, the fight was over. Frank was dying in the street. Billy and Tom, still alive, were carried into a house. As Dr. William Millar gave Billy morphine, Billy said, "They have murdered me. I have been murdered. Chase the crowd away from the door and give me air." Then he died. Tom later died as well. When coroner Henry Mathews arrived, he found no gun or cartridges on Tom's body.[46]

I began my research accepting the Earp explanation of the gun-fight, but after reviewing the testimony from the coroner's inquest and the hearing before Judge Wells Spicer, I believe that the Clantons and McLaurys were in the process of ending their business in town and leaving, not looking for a confrontation with the Earps and Doc Holliday. I believe that Tom was unarmed when opening his coat and that the other Cowboys had their hands in the air when Doc Holliday and Morgan Earp fired the first two shots—and the rest is history.

Chapter Two

THE JAMES-YOUNGER GANG RAID ON THE NORTHFIELD BANK

JUST THE FACTS

"MY! HOW THOSE FELLOWS CAN RIDE. JUST LIKE PRUSSIAN SOLDIERS," William Ebel overheard Ferdinand Burke marvel as a group of strangers rode into Northfield, Minnesota, early in the morning on Thursday, September 7, 1876. Ebel later saw the same men carousing in a saloon.[1] That morning, eight members of the James-Younger Gang had entered Northfield from different directions at different times intent on robbing Northfield's First National Bank.

Historians dispute some of the gang members' identities and their number. Bob, Jim, and Cole Younger, later captured, were gang members, as well as Clell Miller, Charlie Pitts, and Bill Chadwell, who were killed. The James brothers denied being involved, and the Youngers refused to name them, but many believe they were involved. Researchers dispute whether it was Jesse or Frank James who entered the First National Bank. Cole Younger said the robber in the bank was a man named Howard and the outside man's name was Woods.[2] Jesse often used the alias "Howard" and Frank was known to use the alias "Woodson."[3] Let's stick with Howard and Woods for this telling. There are many versions as to what happened—here is ours.

By two o'clock that afternoon, Howard, Bob Younger, and Charlie Pitts tied their horses to hitching posts on Division Street, near the bank. Cole Younger and Clell Miller rode up from the south. Meanwhile, Woods, Jim Younger, and Bill Chadwell waited nearby on horseback at the Cannon River bridge.

A vault stood inside the bank, housing a safe with a time lock designed to only open at predetermined times. On the morning of the raid, the vault door was open and the safe's door closed but unlocked, with $15,000 available for transactions.[4] Three employees worked in the bank: Joseph Heywood, bookkeeper and acting cashier; Frank Wilcox, assistant bookkeeper; and Alonzo Bunker, a teller.

As three men entered the bank, Bunker thought they were customers until he saw revolvers pointed at him.

"Throw up your hands for we intend to rob this bank and if you holler we will blow your God damned brains out," one robber said.[5] Heywood sat in the cashier's chair. Another robber said to him, "I know you're the cashier. Now open the safe damn quick or I'll blow your head off."[6]

As Charlie Pitts began entering the vault, Heywood tried to close the vault door on him. The other robbers dragged Heywood away, shoving their revolvers in his face, saying, "Open that safe, now, or you haven't a minute to live."[7]

"There is a time lock on, and it cannot be opened," Heywood replied. The robbers told him again to open the safe. One of them drew his knife across Heywood's throat with enough pressure to make Heywood bleed. Heywood shouted, "Murder!" and was struck on the head, knocking him to the floor. Demanding that he open the safe, Pitts fired his revolver close to Heywood's head, but he still refused to obey.[8]

The robbers had failed to close the outside bank door. Clell Miller and Cole Younger dismounted. As Miller walked to the door, closing it, store owner J. S. Allen approached. Miller grabbed him, saying, "You son of a bitch, don't you holler." Allen broke away, screaming, "Get your guns, boys. They are robbing the bank!" as medical student Henry Wheeler shouted, "Robbery! They are robbing the bank!" Miller shot at Wheeler, shouting, "Get back or I'll kill you!"[9]

Wheeler ran across the street to the Dampier Hotel, borrowed a carbine and ammunition, and bounded up the stairs to a third-floor window overlooking the street.

Cole Younger shot at people, screaming, "Get in you son of a bitch!" as Woods, Chadwell, and Jim Younger galloped into Division Street shooting and yelling.[10]

Allen ran to his store, where he dispensed weapons and ammunition to townsmen. Elias Stacy took a shotgun loaded with birdshot and blasted Miller in the face as he was mounting his horse. Miller was hurt and dazed but still alive. Anselm Manning borrowed a rifle from a store display window and proceeded to shoot Pitts's horse.

Wheeler then shot Miller in the chest, killing him. As Cole Younger ran to Miller's aid, Manning fired again, hitting Younger's left hip. Bloodied, Cole mounted and rode to the bank, shouting to his comrades, "Come out of the bank!"[11]

Manning continued firing, killing Chadwell. Jim Younger was hit in the shoulder by a bullet.

Inside the bank, Bob Younger was gathering money from the counter and drawers. Alonzo Bunker made a break for it as Pitts shot at him. The bank employee ran out the back door and was crossing an empty lot when Pitts shot him in the right shoulder, but he kept running.

Cole yelled into the bank, "For God's sake come out! They are shooting us all to pieces!"[12]

Nellie Ames, whose husband was a part owner of the bank, stood in the intersection of Fifth and Division Streets. "Lady, get off the street or you will be killed!" Cole shouted as he saw Nicolaus Gustavson, a drunken Swede, weaving toward him. Without hesitation, Cole shot Gustavson in the head.[13]

Bob Younger, followed by Pitts and Howard, ran out of the bank. The last robber shot Heywood in the head, killing him. Cole said that Pitts shot Heywood. Six years later, Wilcox identified Frank James as the shooter. Or was it Jesse?

Anselm Manning and Bob Younger engaged in a shoot-out, each trying to get a clear shot at the other. Wheeler shot at Younger, hitting his right elbow.

As bullets continued to fly, the six remaining gang members mounted their horses, Bob riding double with Cole, and galloped south out of town.

Joseph Heywood sacrificed his life protecting the First National Bank's money. The bank offered a $500 reward for the bandits' capture and established a fund for Heywood's family. The public was outraged at the paltry reward, so the bank quickly raised it to $3,000. Adelbert Ames, a major investor in the bank, contributed $1,000, lamenting to his wife Blanche, "This would buy the much-coveted stem-winding watch—and—well, I have forgotten what the other thing is I stand so much in need of."[14]

SOUTHERN VENGEANCE——BILL MARKLEY

The Civil War begat the James-Younger Gang. Frank and Jesse James, along with Cole, Bob, and Jim Younger, became legends. Newspapers, dime novels, and books exaggerated their exploits, proclaiming them Robin Hood characters robbing the rich and helping the poor. The James and Younger boys were masters at eluding posses and providing alibis. The Civil War never ended for the gang members, who continued to exact revenge on hated Yankee interests—Yankee banks and Yankee railroads—ultimately leading to the gang's demise at Northfield, Minnesota, on September 7, 1876.

The Civil War in Missouri started long before shots were fired at Fort Sumter, South Carolina, on April 12, 1861. Many slave owners and slaves lived in adjacent counties along the Missouri River known as Little Dixie. Missouri became divided between proslavery and abolitionist parties, heated arguments and strident newspaper editorials degenerated into fistfights and brawls, descending into theft, destruction, intimidation, and murder. Both sides organized militias to protect their members and attack opponents. Proslavery bands were called Bushwhackers or Border Ruffians, and abolitionist bands were named Jayhawkers. Open warfare erupted in 1855, continuing into the onslaught of the Civil War and for years afterward.

This constant warfare influenced the James brothers—Frank, born in 1843, and Jesse, born in 1847—as they grew up in Clay County, Missouri, part of Little Dixie. The boys received a good education from their stepfather, Dr. Ruben Samuels, and mother, Zerelda James, prosperous farmers. Ruben and Zerelda were proslavery and owned slaves who worked alongside the family at day-to-day chores.

Frank joined the local pro-Southern Missouri State Guard on May 4, 1861, while Jesse remained on the farm. Frank participated in several Civil War battles but was captured while recuperating from measles in a hospital. He was paroled and released; however, he soon joined a local guerrilla group and later William Quantrill's Bushwhackers.[15]

On May 25, 1863, Frank's Bushwhacker outfit visited the family farm for a meal and rest, setting up camp in some nearby woods. Jesse was working with one of the farmhands in the tobacco fields when local Unionist militia caught and whipped him. They took him to the house, where they interrogated the family as to the whereabouts of Frank and the other Bushwhackers. The Unionists tied a rope around Dr. Samuels's neck, tossed the other end over a tree limb, and hoisted him off the ground, strangling him. They then dropped Samuels to the ground; still alive, he revealed the Bushwhacker hiding place. The troops ambushed the camp, but Frank escaped. The militia men jailed Samuels and Zerelda James, who were released only after signing loyalty oaths. At this point Jesse became hell-bent in his hatred of Yankees.[16]

In 1864, Jesse joined Frank with Fletch Taylor's Bushwhackers and later "Bloody Bill" Anderson's men, who were noted for atrocities and murder. After Bloody Bill was killed, the brothers split, joining separate Bushwhacker groups. On May 15, 1865, with the war officially over, Jesse and other Bushwhackers were surrendering when they were attacked. Jesse was shot through a lung but eventually recovered.[17]

Even though the Civil War was over, the brothers remained at war, joining Bushwhacker groups who were raiding banks. It's difficult to determine what bank jobs the James brothers were associated with, as they were good at covering their tracks, and Jesse was good at writing to newspapers denying involvement in the robberies. Missouri newspaper editor John Edwards became a staunch supporter of the two, meeting the James brothers, writing editorials in their defense, and publishing Jesse's letters.[18]

The James brothers (Frank sitting, Jesse standing on the right) and Charles Fletcher Taylor (standing on the left). COURTESY OF THE STATE HISTORICAL SOCIETY OF MISSOURI

The James brothers, along with the Younger brothers, robbed their first train on July 21, 1873, derailing a Rock Island train near Adair, Iowa, and stealing more than $2,000.[19] The boys now concentrated their efforts mostly on trains transporting large amounts of cash owned by Northern interests. To many Missourians, the railroads represented Northern treachery and greed.

In 1874, the Adams Express Company, whose money was stolen during the Rock Island train holdup, hired the Pinkerton National Detective Agency, headquartered in Chicago, to stop the James-Younger Gang.[20] After one of their agents was found dead near the James farm, Pinkerton detectives raided the Jameses' homestead on the night of January 25, 1875. Hoping to flush out Frank and Jesse, detectives threw a bomb through a window and into the house; it exploded, killing the Jameses' young half-brother, Archie, and mangling one of Zerelda's arms.[21] Jesse and Frank were not home at the time. The raid outraged Missourians, and the state legislature almost passed an amnesty bill for Frank and Jesse.[22]

The war in Missouri had also bitterly affected the Younger boys—Cole, born in 1844, and his younger brothers Jim and Bob. Their parents, Henry and Bursheba, had fourteen children, who received the best education available at the time. The Younger family was prosperous, owning two farms, a dry goods store, and slaves in Jackson County, Missouri. Although he was a slave owner, Henry did not support secession. He held the US government contract for mail service for five hundred miles of territory. Socially prominent, Henry was elected to the Missouri legislature three times and served as county judge.[23]

As violence escalated between the abolitionists and proslavery sympathizers, Jayhawkers ransacked Henry's store and disrupted the mail service. Henry visited the pro-Union Missouri militia headquarters in Kansas City, requesting that they stop the marauders. On his way home, Henry was ambushed and murdered by the Missouri militia, who believed that Henry had a large amount of money on him.[24]

Union troops imprisoned three Younger sisters and two female cousins, along with other proslavery women, in an old two-story house in Kansas City. The house collapsed, killing many of the inmates, including one of the Younger cousins. Cole and others believed that Jayhawkers had deliberately undermined the foundations to collapse the structure.[25]

At seventeen, Cole joined William Quantrill's Bushwhackers, participating in fights and atrocities, including the massacre of more than two hundred men and boys at Lawrence, Kansas. It was while riding with Quantrill that Cole formed a lasting friendship with Frank James. The attacks on the Younger family continued. The Unionist Missouri militia forced Bursheba to burn down her own house and then ordered her and the four youngest children to trudge eight miles through the snow to find shelter. Cole believed that the constant persecution of his mother led to her death on October 6, 1870.[26]

Cole continued his Bushwhacker activities after the war, joining the Jameses and later involving his brothers Bob, John, and Jim in bank and train robberies. On March 17, 1874, Pinkerton agents killed John Younger in a gun battle.[27] Cole and his surviving brothers would always hold a grudge against Pinkerton agents.

Clell Miller came from a prosperous slave-owning family in Clay County near the Jameses. He joined Bloody Bill Anderson's Bushwhackers at the age of fourteen. On October 27, 1864, Bloody Bill was shot and killed and Clell was wounded and captured. The Unionists were about to execute him when Lieutenant Colonel Samuel Cox, an old friend of Clell's father, recognized him. Clell claimed that he had been forced to join Bloody Bill. So Cox spared Clell, sending him to prison in St. Louis. Clell remained a close friend of Jesse's and a dependable James-Younger Gang member.[28]

Charlie Pitts, whose real name was Samuel Wells, lived near and was good friends with the Younger family. When Charlie was fourteen years old, he and his mother found Henry Younger's body. Two months later, Charlie's father, a civilian, was shot and killed while cheering on the Confederates at the battle of White Oak Creek. Charlie joined the Bushwhackers, but little is known of his activities. He married after the war and moved to Kansas. Charlie loved women, having at least two affairs. His jilted lovers disclosed to the authorities and newspapers that Charlie was in league with the Youngers and Jameses in bank and train robberies.[29]

Bill Chadwell was born in 1853 in Greene County, Illinois. After his father died, the family moved to southeastern Kansas. People said that he was easily influenced. Bill was good friends with Charlie Pitts and allegedly participated in several bank and railroad robberies with the James-Younger Gang.[30]

On July 7, 1876, the James-Younger Gang robbed the Missouri Pacific Railroad at Rocky Cut, Missouri. Authorities caught gang member Hobbs Kerry, who broke after being interrogated, naming gang members Bill Chadwell, Charlie Pitts, Clell Miller, Cole Younger, Bob Younger, Frank James, and Jesse James.[31] Jesse sent letters to the newspapers declaring Kerry a liar and appealed to old Missouri Confederates, stating that he was being persecuted for his loyalty to the South.

The gang learned that the hated Yankee Republican Adelbert Ames now lived in Northfield, Minnesota. They decided Ames and his money would be their next target and headed north into Yankee territory.

Adelbert Ames moved to Northfield, Minnesota, in May 1876. His father and brother were prominent citizens, owning Northfield's flour mill and a fourth of Northfield's First National Bank. Adelbert, a New Englander, had graduated from West Point in George Armstrong Custer's class. He was a Civil War hero, receiving the Congressional Medal of Honor, and rose through the ranks to general. After the war, during Reconstruction, Adelbert moved to Mississippi, where the Radical Republicans and blacks elected him to the Senate and then to the office of governor. During the 1875 election, the Democrats intimidated Republicans and blacks. Riots broke out. People were injured, murders were committed, and voters were barred from the polls throughout Mississippi.

After the election, the Democrats gained control of the legislature and began impeachment proceedings against Ames on trumped-up charges. At the suggestion of his wife, Blanche, Adelbert resigned to save face, but not before the charges were leaked to the newspapers. Even though Adelbert did not live in Missouri and had done nothing to harm Missourians, the Missouri newspapers blasted him as a symbol of Northern tyranny and corruption.[32]

Arriving in Northfield in 1876, Adelbert joined his father and brother in managing their mill while his wife, Blanche, the beautiful, influential daughter of the infamous General Benjamin Butler, remained in New England. When Adelbert and Blanche had married in 1870, Butler had staged a three-day celebration, with enough dignitaries present to resemble "a chapter out of the Arabian Nights."[33] Adelbert Ames was a hated name in the South, second only to his father-in-law.

New England lawyer and politician General Benjamin Butler had led Union troops into New Orleans on May 1, 1862, after its surrender. He received the moniker "Beast Butler" after issuing General Order No. 28, which stated that any woman who insulted a Union officer would "be treated as a woman of the town plying her avocation"—in other words, a prostitute. Butler's order horrified Southerners.[34] Then, on June 7, 1862, Butler had William Mumford hanged for tearing down an American flag.[35]

Scandal clouded Butler's management of New Orleans. Many believed that he stole private property, nicknaming him "Spoons." Not only did Butler's staff and his brother Andrew make money in confiscated cotton and goods, but Butler profited as well.[36]

After hearing evidence of Butler's mismanagement of New Orleans, President Abraham Lincoln placed General Nathaniel Banks in command over Butler. Resenting the snub, Butler resigned.[37] He was elected to Congress as a Radical Republican who helped lead the charge to impeach President Andrew Johnson and punish the South. By 1876, Butler had accumulated a vast amount of wealth.

The James-Younger Gang converged on Saint Paul, Minnesota, buying fine horses and visiting towns near Northfield, thirty-nine miles south of Saint Paul. They knew the Ames family members were major investors in the First National Bank, and, best of all, they could punish not only Ames but also Spoons Butler. Cole Younger later stated, "We had been informed that ex-Governor Ames of Mississippi and General Benjamin Butler of Massachusetts had deposited $75,000 in the National Bank."[38]

On September 29, 1872, John Edwards, in an editorial in the *Kansas City Times* titled "The Chivalry of Crime," alluding to the James-Younger Gang, wrote, "But there are things done for money and for revenge of which the daring of the act is the picture and the crime the frame that it be set in. [A] feat of stupendous nerve and fearlessness that makes one's hair rise to think of it, with a condiment of crime to season it, becomes chivalric, poetic, superb."[39]

CRIME OF OPPORTUNITY—KELLEN CUTSFORTH

Over the decades, the name Jesse James has made its way into infamy. Perhaps no other outlaw, outside of Billy the Kid, has made such a lasting mark on the history books. And, like most of the subjects in this book, myth and mystery shroud the life of this famous desperado and the bandit gang with which he rode.

Jesse's motivations behind the myriad of crimes he committed with his brother Frank; Cole, Jim, John, and Bob Younger; and several other confidants have always come into question. Through the years, and even at the height of the James-Younger Gang's activities, much of the public saw Jesse and his brethren as Robin Hoods who were stealing from rich Northerners and giving back to the poor. In fact, former president Harry S. Truman in 1949, while in his home state of Missouri, said, "Jesse James was a modern-day Robin Hood. He stole from the rich and gave to the poor, which, in general, is not a bad policy."[40]

Of course, the idea of Jesse or any of his band as Southern Robin Hoods has been found to be total bunk. Over the years, many historians have proven, through meticulous research, that the James-Younger Gang took part in a dozen bank heists, seven train robberies, and four stagecoach holdups. These activities resulted in at least a dozen murders and injured around ten people. Most of these robberies took place in the James-Younger Gang's home state of Missouri. Throughout all of this, there is absolutely no evidence that a single cent found its way into the hands of any impoverished people.[41]

Along with the multitude of lies about his giving nature and attempts at redistribution of wealth, even the death of Jesse James has come into question. Some believe that the youngest James brother did not meet his end by way of an assassin's bullet but lived on to old age, much like Billy the Kid. Unlike the Kid, however, there are photographs of James's stiff cadaver, and the body was displayed for a time so that people who viewed him could enjoy a bit of macabre entertainment. Furthermore, in 1995 the body of Jesse was exhumed and DNA testing was performed on the corpse. The results revealed that the dead body's DNA was consistent with that known to be Jesse James's.[42] This test debunked yet another James-Younger myth.

Further examination of the James-Younger Gang's exploits brings to light an additional myth surrounding Jesse and his partners. The attempted robbery of the First National Bank of Northfield, Minnesota, in 1876 (historically known as the Northfield Raid) is a moment in the chronicles of the Old West that continues to gild the reputation of the James-Younger Gang. Almost from the advent of their high-risk heists, the James and Younger boys became heroes of the fallen Confederacy.

The Northfield Raid on September 7, 1876, saw the James-Younger Gang try to rob the First National Bank of Northfield around two o'clock in the afternoon. The gang ran into an onslaught of heavily armed citizens who were intent on not allowing the gang to escape with their life savings. After a fierce gun battle and ensuing manhunt, all but Jesse and Frank James were either dead or captured. That bloody day in Northfield destroyed the James-Younger Gang for good.[43]

Through the years, the gang had collected several members who had been sympathetic to the cause of the Confederacy during the Civil War. Referencing Jesse's Confederate sympathies, noted historian Richard Slotkin said, "James's turn to crime after the end of the Reconstruction era helped cement his place in American life and memory as a simple but remarkably effective bandit. After 1873 he was covered by the national media as part of social banditry."[44] It is true that during the gang's height they were celebrated chiefly by former Confederates. Contemporary historians have referred to the gang as social bandits or members of the lower class struggling against the ruling class through illegal means.[45]

It can be argued that the James-Younger Gang's motivations, however, were less noble then the championing of a failed cause, especially when it came to the Northfield Raid. To better understand the raid, one must examine the events leading up to it. Although many Confederate sympathizers sided with the James-Youngers, the gang cared little about the fallen Confederacy.

It is true that many of the gang members were former Bushwhackers and rebel soldiers. Some of these men participated in atrocities committed upon antislavery towns (such as the massacre at Lawrence, Kansas, and the massacre of Union soldiers at Centralia, Missouri), but when they began robbing banks, they targeted depositories mostly in Missouri, a state with strong ties to the Confederacy. These banks were in business long before there was ever any Federal Deposit Insurance Corporation; if you lost your money to bandits who robbed the bank, you lost your money in whole. So the James-Youngers were basically stealing from people who were sympathetic toward them.

Cole and Bob Younger later stated that they selected the First National Bank in Northfield because they believed that it was associated with the Republican politician Adelbert Ames, the governor of Mississippi during Reconstruction, and with Union general Benjamin Butler, Ames's father-in-law and the former Union commander of occupied New Orleans. Ames was a stockholder in the bank, though Butler had no direct connection to it.[46] In reality, however, this belief had no bearing on the James-Younger Gang's decision to rob the Northfield bank.

The true reason the James-Younger Gang rode into Minnesota was not to deliver a punishing blow to the land of Yankees and Northern aggression but to exact individual vengeance. In January 1875, the James-Younger Gang had committed so many crimes, including murder, that they were being pursued by the Pinkerton National Detective Agency. The agency was founded by Allan Pinkerton in 1850. The Pinkerton agents performed services ranging from security guards to private military contracting work.

The Pinkertons were hired to end the James-Younger Gang's reign of terror, and in January 1875 they set their sights on the James family farm in Clay County, Missouri. A man named Samuel Hardwicke, an attorney who was also Allan Pinkerton's right-hand man, helped launch the assault. The Pinkerton men knew that there were innocent people inside and that neither of the James boys were at the farm, but they attacked it anyway.[47]

This onslaught consisted of the Pinkerton agents surrounding the James farmhouse and tossing an incendiary device into the home. The following explosion killed young Archie Samuels, Jesse's half-brother, and maimed his mother, Zerelda, blowing off her arm.[48] About the brutality of the attack, Pinkerton said, "Above everything, destroy the [James] house, blot it from the face of the earth."[49] Hardwicke was part of the plot to blot out the home from the earth, and the James boys knew it.

Seven days after the attack on the farmhouse, the *Chicago Tribune* ran an article exposing Hardwicke as a Pinkerton operative. The story was picked up by the Missouri press, which readily informed the James brothers. Through correspondence from Hardwicke and other sources, Jesse believed that Hardwicke was the key instigator in the death of his young half-brother Archie and the crippling of his mother.[50]

Along with Samuel Hardwicke, the James boys found out that their mother's neighbor Daniel Askew was also working as a Pinkerton agent. After discovering this information, Jesse surprised Askew outside his home. Three shots sounded from Jesse's pistol, nearly blowing off Askew's head.[51] After the violent death of Askew, the *Kansas City Times* commented on the murder, writing, "There is a tiger loose in Clay County and no man can say who will be the next victim."[52]

These articles and Askew's death frightened the men who had conspired with Allan Pinkerton to kill the James brothers' family and destroy their home. In fact, one Missouri paper included a list of five men who had conspired with the Pinkertons, and one of the men on the list was Samuel Hardwicke.[53]

Knowing that he was clearly on the James boys' hit list, in the darkness of night in May 1876, Hardwicke and his family boarded a train. After a two-day ride, the family stepped off the train in Saint Paul, Minnesota.[54] No more than three months after Hardwicke arrived in Minnesota, the James-Younger Gang met to discuss their future.[55] At this meeting, Jesse stepped to the forefront and suggested that they make their way to Minnesota. All the gang members knew this was Jesse looking for vengeance, plain and simple.[56]

Most historians believe Jesse convinced the gang members to head to Minnesota because they would have freedom of movement and no one would expect them to operate that far north. These historians also believe that Jesse told the gang there would be brothels and casinos in the large cities of Saint Paul and Minneapolis and easy money to be had from the loosely guarded banks in the area.[57] The gang also felt that by pulling a bank heist so far north, the Pinkertons and their ilk would be drawn away from the gang's usual hideouts in Missouri.[58]

This was all a ruse by Jesse to get his gang into Minnesota so that he could exact retribution for the brutality inflicted on his family. The infiltration of Northern states had nothing to do with old Bushwhackers waging war with the Union, and everything to do with the fulfillment of a vendetta. Jesse wanted Hardwicke dead.

So when it came to the First National Bank of Northfield and the ensuing raid perpetrated by the James-Younger Gang, it was nothing more than a crime of opportunity. Jesse wanted the gang in Minnesota so that he could kill Hardwicke, just as he had killed Askew. Hardwicke had been so witless and felt so safe that he wrote an editorial to the *Liberty Tribune* in Missouri, giving away his Saint Paul address.[59] This act felt like a taunt to Jesse and enraged him even more—as if he needed the motivation. In fact, while in Saint Paul, Jesse referred to his intention to kill Hardwicke when he told a local prostitute that his guns were for "a man that he knew up town."[60]

Author and historian Mark Lee Gardner, when referring to the gang's intentions for the Northfield bank, has said it best: "Minnesota offered lots of fat banks, many of them easy marks, with the potential for a big haul."[61] The First National Bank of Northfield was "low hanging fruit" to the James-Younger Gang. And it was ripe for the picking. There was no rebel pride to be had by hitting the bank; it was pure opportunism.

When the gang raided the First National Bank, however, they bit off more than they could chew. They did not count on the people of Northfield defending what was theirs. When the town's people arrived heavily armed and prepared for a fight to ensure the safety of their life savings, it was too much for the James-Younger boys to handle. With the destruction of their gang, the deaths and capture of multiple members, and the eventual death of Jesse, the myth of Old West Robin Hoods and a fight for the Southern cause was destroyed as well.

Chapter Three

WILD BILL HICKOK— SHOWDOWN AT ROCK CREEK STATION

JUST THE FACTS

WILD BILL HICKOK BECAME A NATIONAL CELEBRITY AFTER COLONEL George Ward Nichols wrote of his exploits in the January 1867 issue of *Harper's New Monthly Magazine*. The public considered Wild Bill a hero after learning that he had single-handedly defeated the murderous McCanles gang at Rock Creek Station, Nebraska Territory, on July 12, 1861.

Nichols told how David McCanles, captain of a gang of border ruffians, was out to get Wild Bill after he beat McCanles in wrestling and shooting matches. One day, McCanles and nine gang members trapped Wild Bill in a cabin on Rock Creek. Nichols wrote about the incident in Wild Bill's words:

> *"Surround the house and give him no quarter!" Yelled M'Kandlas [sic]. . . . He jumped inside the room with his gun leveled to shoot; but he was not quick enough. My rifle-ball went through his heart. He fell back outside the house . . . [Wild Bill grabbed his pistols and] the ruffians came rushing at both doors. How wild they looked with their red, drunken faces and inflamed eyes, shouting and cussing! But I never aimed more deliberately in my life.*

One-two-three-four; and four men fell dead.

That didn't stop the rest. Two of them fired their bird guns at me. . . . One I knocked down with my fist. . . . The second I shot dead. The other three clutched me and crowded me onto the bed. I fought hard. I broke with my hand one man's arm. He had his fingers round my throat. Before I got to my feet I was struck across the breast with the stock of a rifle. . . . Then I got ugly, and I remember that I got hold of a knife, and then it was all cloudy like, and I was wild, and I struck savage blows, following the devils up from one side to the other of the room and into the corners, striking and slashing until I knew every one [sic] was dead."[1]

J. W. Buel told a slightly different version of the story in his 1881 book, *Heroes of the Plains*,[2] and Buffalo Bill Cody repeated the story, adding that McCanles had murdered Cody's father during the Kansas troubles.[3]

Some people hated Wild Bill, while others loved him. He worked as a scout and a law enforcement officer. He loved to gamble and tell tall tales. He could be kind and he could be coldhearted, but he had a strong sense of justice. He was an excellent shot, constantly practicing. Nichols wrote in his 1867 magazine story that Hickok had killed hundreds of men,[4] while Hickok claimed to have killed thirty-six men, though his documented killings stand at seven.[5] (Hickok's number of thirty-six probably includes men he killed during the Civil War and in Indian fights.)

Elizabeth Custer, General George Armstrong Custer's wife, wrote of Hickok, "Physically he was a delight to look upon. Tall, lithe, and free in every motion, he rode and walked as if every muscle was perfection."[6]

Wild Bill was born James Butler Hickok on May 27, 1837, in Troy Grove, Illinois. At an early age, he loved guns and hunting. His strong sense of justice originated with his parents, both active in the Underground Railroad, assisting slaves in their quest for freedom. When his father died, Hickok and his brothers worked to support the family by farming, hunting, and taking odd jobs. One such job, working as a driver for the Illinois and Michigan Canal, was abruptly terminated after

Hickok caught his employer mistreating horses and threw him in the canal.[7]

Hickok and his brother Lorenzo headed to Kansas in the 1850s to find a homestead and make their fortune. They farmed and worked at a variety of jobs. Lorenzo returned home, but Hickok stayed in Kansas. At this time, tensions began heating up between proslavery and antislavery factions. Hickok joined the Free State Army, an antislavery group, and participated in actions against proslavery supporters.[8]

In 1857, Hickok met eleven-year-old William F. Cody, who would become a lifelong friend later known as Buffalo Bill. Cody claimed they worked for the freighting company Russell, Majors and Waddell, hauling army supplies by bull train during the Mormon War (1857–1858). Cody said their bull train was captured by Mormon raiders, who burned the wagons with their supplies.[9] The only record of this adventure, however, is in Cody's autobiography. What is certain is that by 1858 Cody was already friends with the older Hickok.[10]

From 1858 to 1861, Hickok worked for the freighting company Jones and Cartwright.[11] On March 22, 1858, he was elected Montello Township constable.[12] In the fall of 1860, he was severely injured (some claimed in a bear attack). He began work in Nebraska at Russell, Majors and Waddell's Pony Express Rock Creek Relay Station in the spring of 1861, tending horses as his injuries healed. It was at the Rock Creek Station that events were set in motion, propelling James Hickok to national fame as Wild Bill.

A CASE FOR SELF-DEFENSE—KELLEN CUTSFORTH

As the route of the Pony Express wound its way from St. Joseph, Missouri, through Kansas Territory, and eventually north, the famous mail route's first stop in what is now the state of Nebraska was known as Rock Creek Station. It was here that James Butler "Wild Bill" Hickok, arguably the country's greatest gunfighter, forged his reputation.

Rock Creek Station, located in southern Nebraska near the town of Fairbury, was not only on the Pony Express line but also a stagecoach stop.[13] Hickok came to work at Rock Creek in late April or May 1861

Wild Bill Hickok. New York photographer George Rockwood took this photograph circa 1873. COURTESY OF DENVER PUBLIC LIBRARY, WESTERN HISTORY COLLECTION (Z-8870)

as a stable hand, most likely for the Russell, Majors and Waddell Company, the owner and operators of the Pony Express.[14]

While in Rock Creek, Hickok encountered David McCanles. Reported to be six feet tall and heavily built, McCanles was a rough character with questionable associations.[15] In 1859, after abandoning his family in North Carolina and fleeing west to Nebraska Territory with his mistress, Sarah Shull, McCanles settled in Rock Creek, near a small relay station positioned on the Oregon Trail.[16] He eventually bought the station, most likely with funds swindled from Watauga County, North Carolina (a county he was formerly the sheriff of).[17] He soon made improvements to the property.

After developing the property, McCanles bizarrely sent for his family in North Carolina and kept Shull on as a "domestic" (meaning a housekeeper), according to census records.[18] Whatever the case, David McCanles and his family owned the station and in April 1861 were approached by the Russell, Majors and Waddell–owned Central Overland California and Pike's Peak Express Company to sell the eastside ranch for use as a relay station for the fledgling Pony Express.[19] McCanles was given a one-third down payment for the property, with the rest to be doled out over the following three months.[20]

It was not long, however, before tensions began to boil over between McCanles and the Pony Express employees, which included Hickok. It is reported that McCanles did not like Hickok from the onset and took every occasion to humiliate him. He would often throw Hickok to the ground when there were crowds of men present. McCanles also had several nicknames he used to ridicule Hickok, including "Dutch Bill."[21] This nickname has been misinterpreted over the years as "Duck Bill" in supposed reference to Hickok's aquiline nose.[22]

By June 1861, Russell, Majors and Waddell and the Pony Express were on the brink of bankruptcy. In fact, circumstances became so dire for the enterprise that employees of the company began referring to Russell, Majors and Waddell as the "Cleaned out and Poor Pay Outfit."[23]

Seeing the wobbly financial situation of the Pony Express, McCanles began repeatedly arriving at Rock Creek Station demanding payment on the outstanding bill for the property sale from Pony Express superintendent Horace Wellman. Wellman, who was not responsible for the company's defaulting on the debt, had extended and excited conversations with McCanles about the outstanding payment.[24] As an agent for the Pony Express, Wellman lived on the Rock Creek property with his common-law wife, Jane Wellman.[25]

Further complicating matters, Horace Wellman's father-in-law, Joseph Holmes, who was also living near the Rock Creek property, was at some point accused by McCanles of stealing his property. On July 5, 1861, McCanles caught up to Holmes and apparently beat him severely. To what extent and with what methods the beating ensued are not completely clear.[26] But the beating was bad enough that Jane Wellman despised McCanles for it and did not trust his intentions from that day forward.[27]

Before this event, however, on July 1, Horace Wellman left with McCanles's twelve-year-old son Monroe for Brownville, Nebraska Territory, to make an inquiry with the Pony Express division office there about acquiring the money for the remaining payments to McCanles.[28] When Horace and Monroe returned from their trip on the afternoon of July 11, they found tensions at a boiling point. Wellman informed McCanles that Benjamin Ficklin, the Pony Express line superintendent in Brownville, could not promise any money or a date of payment.[29] This information did not sit well with McCanles.

It is generally believed that McCanles, once he had the money from the sale of Rock Creek Station, was looking to pull up roots again and head for the western wilderness.[30] His anxiousness over leaving the Rock Creek area was due in part to his violent and threatening nature. Many of the settlers in the area showed a great deal of hostility toward McCanles because he had mistreated several of them, not just Wellman's family and Hickok. McCanles believed that most of the inhabitants of the Rock Creek area would welcome his downfall.[31] McCanles was a brute, as evidenced by how he dealt with Jane Wellman's father and his bullying of Hickok. It is no wonder that many of the locals were afraid of him.

So, on the afternoon of July 12, the day of Wellman's return, McCanles came to Rock Creek Station. This time he made the journey with his son Monroe, and two cohorts, James Woods and James Gordon, tagged along.[32] More than likely, McCanles was enraged, looking for his money and looking for a fight. It is at this point that a great deal of controversy and conjecture surrounding this famous historic event arises.

Most defenders of David McCanles (and, by extension, Woods and Gordon) say that the men were unarmed and only looking to recoup the money owed for the sale of Rock Creek Station. It is a fact, however, that McCanles made a habit of going armed wherever he traveled and especially on the occasions when he made the trek to the Rock Creek property. He normally brought two revolvers with him and a short double-barreled shotgun, which he usually carried on his saddle horn.[33]

It is also important to note that highly respected Wild Bill Hickok historians William E. Connelley and Joseph G. Rosa both find it quite peculiar and out of place for a man like McCanles to show up unarmed at a place where he had previously engaged in confrontations with the employees and their families. In fact, Rosa wrote about the fight, "It does seem odd that for a man who normally went armed, McCanles, determined to retrieve by force if necessary what he still regarded as his property, should be unarmed."[34]

The accepted scenario at this juncture has McCanles dismounting from his horse, along with his son, and approaching Horace Wellman, who, after entering into a brief argument over the outstanding debt and ownership of the station, retreated into the property's two-room dwelling, where he and his wife were staying.[35] As Wellman entered the home, his wife, Jane, began to berate McCanles for beating her father.[36] At this point, Hickok arrived, and after a brief exchange, McCanles asked him for a drink of water. Hickok then entered the home, apparently to retrieve the water.

After Hickok entered the house, history once again becomes hazy. Many historians claim that after Hickok walked indoors he was confronted by a scared and anxious Wellman, causing him to draw his two pistols. Wellman then armed himself with a rifled musket, which ironically had been loaned to him by McCanles.[37] The small home was divided by a curtain hanging from a clothesline, which, it is alleged, Wellman and Hickok stood behind as McCanles approached the south doorway.[38]

It was at this point that McCanles was hit with a rifle ball, most likely fired by Wellman and not by Hickok. The bullet drove him backward out of the entryway and onto his back, where he died. Wild Bill, fearing that Woods and Gordon were armed, sprang into action with his pair of pistols and began firing at them. Both were wounded, but Woods fell and was set upon by Jane Wellman, who caved in his head with a gardening hoe. Gordon, however, ran from the fight and into the brush, where he was pursued by Hickok and other Pony Express employees who had arrived on the scene. Gordon was later discovered and killed by a shotgun blast produced by one of the men accompanying Hickok.[39]

Following the ordeal, Hickok, Wellman, and a Pony Express rider named James W. "Doc" Brink, who also had joined in the fight, were arrested for murder and remanded into custody in Beatrice, Nebraska Territory.[40] The men appeared before Justice of the Peace T. M. Coulter, and their hearing took place between July 15, 16, and 18, 1861.[41] They pleaded that their actions were taken in self-defense and in protection of Pony Express company property. After testimony was heard from several individuals, including Jane Wellman, Coulter found that charges of murder against Hickok, Wellman, and Brink were "not sustained" and discharged all three men.[42]

There is no surviving written record from any of the witnesses, including Hickok, concerning this battle. Twelve-year-old Monroe McCanles was not allowed to testify. When evaluating the evidence that does remain from this affair, however, it is easy to make a case for Hickok. Horace Wellman had more reason to kill McCanles than Wild Bill. He also had the rifle used to kill McCanles. Hickok, by contrast, most likely felt that he was defending company property with his actions.[43]

It is true that the *Harper's New Monthly Magazine* article that shed first light on the affair for the public was a complete fabrication. It is total bunk that there was ever a "McCanles gang" or that Hickok squared off against seven or more men on that fateful day in 1861. There is also no proof that Wild Bill was at the station recuperating from a violent encounter with a bear, which has become a part of his legend. Nor can one give much credence to Buffalo Bill Cody's claims that the so-called McCanles gang had killed his father and Wild Bill put an end to them, saving a damsel in distress in the process.[44] This is all legend building, which was often used by frontiersmen of the time, such as Hickok and Cody, to further enhance their already legendary deeds and reputations.

Furthermore, McCanles probably was never a Confederate sympathizer, as he is often accused of being, and he probably never used sadistic punishments to deal with people with whom he had disagreements. McCanles was, however, a bully to people he did not like and who did not agree with him. And he did have an ongoing financial feud with the Pony Express and its parent company, Russell, Majors and Waddell.

McCanles displayed a violent temper and was prone to arguing, especially with the employees at Rock Creek. According to reports, he was always armed with multiple weapons, and deductive reasoning would tell us that he probably also was well armed when he arrived at Rock Creek Station with two of his henchmen in tow on the afternoon of July 12, 1861.

In Horace Wellman, McCanles encountered a man who feared for his life and was going to fight for it. In Wild Bill Hickock, he ran into another man who was not going to be threatened and would defend himself if necessary. No doubt the bloodletting that occurred that day was avoidable and spiraled out of control. But as Justice of the Peace Coulter saw it afterward, the charges of murder against Hickok and the others were unsustainable on the simple grounds of self-defense.

DAVID McCANLES, MISUNDERSTOOD DESPERADO— BILL MARKLEY

Who was David McCanles? What was his gang? And what really happened at Rock Creek Station on July 12, 1861?

David Colbert McCanles was born on November 30, 1828, in Iredell County, North Carolina. His family moved to Watauga County, North Carolina, in the 1830s, when David was a child. He was well educated and had a zest for life. David stood six feet tall with a heavy build. He liked to talk, being considered a good orator, and enjoyed playing practical jokes. He was also competitive, considering himself always right. David enjoyed gambling, racing, wrestling, and bare-knuckle fighting. He married Mary Green in 1848, and through the years they had six children. In 1852, David ran for sheriff of Watauga County in a hotly contested race and won.[45]

The McCanles family lived next door to Phillip and Phoebe Shull, who had thirteen children. Phillip owned and operated Shull's Mill and Shull's Mill Store; Phillip's daughter Sarah, born on October 3, 1833, most likely worked in the store. Sarah was attractive, intelligent, educated, and independent. She became pregnant and had a daughter, Martha Allice Shull, born out of wedlock on May 4, 1856. The community shunned and vilified Sarah and suspected that David was her baby's father. Unfortunately, poor Martha Allice died on July 2, 1857.[46]

In January 1859, David sold his property to his brother and confirmed people's suspicions when, on February 9, 1859, he and Sarah left town together, absconding with tax money belonging to the county. Their plans were to head to Pike's Peak, Colorado, for the latest gold rush. They were traveling along the Oregon Trail through Nebraska Territory to reach the goldfields when they encountered disgruntled returning prospectors who told them it wasn't worth the trip.[47]

The pair reached a way station on the west side of Rock Creek in March 1859. David liked the look of the place and, thinking it might be a profitable business, bought it from the owner.

David began improving Rock Creek Station by building a toll bridge across the creek; on the east side, he built a second house, along with a barn, and dug a well, expanding the water supply.[48] He did quite well with his toll bridge and paid Sarah to manage his financial records.[49]

David sent a letter to his brother James telling him to come to Nebraska Territory and, while he was at it, to bring David's wife and children. And that's exactly what happened. James brought David's family along with a nephew, James Woods. The family lived together in the eastside house, while Sarah lived in the westside house as its housekeeper. David later leased the westside ranch to the Rocky Mountain Dispatch Company. Business boomed, and David had plenty of money, employing twenty men. He developed a ranch three miles southwest of Rock Creek Station, where he moved his family.[50]

David was a respected citizen of Jefferson County, Nebraska Territory. He established the first school in the county and paid the schoolteacher at his own expense (of course, his own children attended). He enjoyed socializing, orating on the latest issues to the delight of his audiences, and he was always popular at dances, playing the fiddle or banjo while singing. David, a staunch Republican, was selected to speak against secession at Jefferson County's 1861 Fourth of July celebration.[51]

He loved practical jokes. One Sunday, a preacher traveling through on the Oregon Trail was giving a sermon at a local ranch house. Unbeknownst to the preacher, David had switched his water glass with one filled with clear moonshine. The preacher took a good healthy drink and began coughing and gagging. The congregation exploded in laughter. When the preacher recovered his breath, he appreciated the joke and parted on friendly terms with David.[52]

In 1860, David made additional improvements, including a bunkhouse at the east ranch. Russell, Majors and Waddell rented it as a relay station for the newly formed Pony Express. Horace Wellman and his common-law wife, Jane, were station managers, and James W. "Doc" Brink was employed as stock tender. In March 1861, James Hickok arrived and worked as assistant stock tender.[53]

David sold the East Rock Creek Station to Russell, Majors and Waddell in April 1861 for one-third the money down and the other two-thirds to be paid in monthly installments through Horace Wellman. David kept the title for security. At this point, the Wellmans were living at the East Rock Creek Station. Sarah had moved to a dugout near David's ranch but assisted Jane at the eastside station.[54]

Russell, Majors and Waddell was in financial trouble. When the company failed to make its June payment, David was upset. Then, when July 1 came and that month's payment was due, Horace Wellman again told David that he could not pay him. Wellman said the superintendent in Brownville, Nebraska Territory, had not sent the money.[55]

David was angry, demanding that he be paid in cash or goods; otherwise, the company needed to return the station to him. He insisted that Wellman travel the long distance to Brownville and come back with an answer. Reluctantly, Wellman did so, leaving on July 2 and taking along David's twelve-year-old son Monroe to pick up supplies for David.[56]

While Wellman was gone, Hickok moved into the eastside station to live.[57] The more David thought about his financial situation, the angrier he became. Several times he went to the eastside station, telling Jane that she needed to get out, but she refused.[58] Jane said that when Horace came home "he would settle" with David for his impudence.[59]

David also believed that Jane's father, Joseph Holmes, had stolen property from him. He caught Holmes on July 5, tied a rope to him, hauled him to the roof of the Rock Creek Station barn, and dropped him over the side to the ground, a process he repeated multiple times. Jane must have witnessed it all.[60]

Horace and Monroe returned to Rock Creek on July 12. Monroe found his father at a nearby ranch and told him that Horace was not able to get cash or supplies for payment. This news infuriated David.[61]

Late that afternoon, David arrived at the East Rock Creek Station with Monroe, his nephew James Woods, and an employee, James Gordon, whose bloodhound tagged along. Dismounting at the barn, Woods and Gordon remained there while David and Monroe walked to the house. Inside were Horace and Jane Wellman, Sarah Shull, Sarah Kelsey, and James Hickok.[62]

David went to the kitchen door, asking for Horace. Jane appeared at the door, and David asked whether Horace was in the house.

"Yes," Jane said.

"Tell him to come out," David said.

"What do you want with him?" she asked.

"I want to settle with him," he answered.

"He'll not come out," she replied.

"Send him out or I'll come in and drag him out," he said.

Hickok stepped to the door, standing beside Jane. David looked him in the face, saying, "Jim, haven't we been friends all the time?"

"Yes," Hickok replied.

"Are we friends now?" David asked.

"Yes."

"Will you hand me a drink of water?" David asked.[63] Hickok turned around to the water bucket and brought a dipper of water, handing it to McCanles. David drank the water, and as he gave the dipper back to Hickok, Monroe noticed that his father saw something threatening take place inside. David moved quickly from the kitchen door to the front door, about ten feet to the north. Stepping onto the front step, David said, "Now, Jim, if you have anything against me, come out and fight me fair." A rifle shot cracked from inside, and David fell flat on his back. He raised himself almost to a sitting position, looked at Monroe, and then fell back dead.[64] Monroe did not see who the shooter was, as the shot came from behind a calico curtain hanging inside the house as a partition.

Sarah Shull later said that she did not see the shooter, as she was standing on the other side of the curtain partition from the shooter. The two Sarahs were ordered to enter the root cellar on the north side of the house and stay there. The roof of the cellar was constructed of split logs.[65]

Hearing the shot, Woods and Gordon came running unarmed to the house. Hickok appeared at the door with a Colt Navy revolver and fired two shots at Woods, who ran around the house to the north.[66]

Gordon turned and ran. Hickok ran after him and fired two shots, wounding him. At the same time, Horace Wellman came outside with a hoe and ran after Woods. Wellman caught Woods over the top of the root cellar, smashing in his head with the hoe.[67] Woods's blood flowed between the split logs down into the root cellar and onto Sarah Shull's head, matting her hair. Shull called it the most horrifying experience of her life.[68]

After killing Woods, Wellman came running back around the house, striking at Monroe with the hoe and yelling, "Let's kill them all!" Monroe dodged the hoe and ran for his life. He outran Wellman to a ravine south of the house and stopped. Jane stood in the doorway, clapping her hands and yelling, "Kill him! Kill him! Kill him!"[69]

The wounded Gordon was hiding down the creek. Doc Brink and a stage driver, George Hulbert, joined Hickok in the hunt for Gordon, putting Gordon's own bloodhound on his trail. The dog found Gordon downstream and either attacked him or was attempting to play with him as Gordon tried to fend him off with a stick. The men then killed Gordon with a shotgun blast.[70]

Returning to the station, Brink, Hulbert, and Hickock met Joe Baker, Sarah Kelsey's stepfather. Hickok accused Baker of being David McCanles's friend and cocked his revolver to kill Baker. But Sarah Kelsey threw her arms around her stepfather, pleading for his life. Hickok relented but said, "Well, you got to take that anyway," as he beat Baker on the head with the barrel of his revolver.[71]

Monroe ran three miles home to tell his mother the horrible news. A hired hand drove her and the children to Rock Creek Station to see for themselves. She sent word to David's brother James, who rode through the night to Beatrice to swear out a murder complaint before Justice of the Peace T. M. Coulter. James McCanles organized a posse, which arrested Hickok, Wellman, and Brink and took them to Beatrice for a preliminary murder hearing.[72]

The morning after the shootings, Frank Thomas and Jasper Helvey went to the station and saw the bodies of David McCanles, James Woods, and James Gordon lying in the positions in which they had fallen. Thomas and Helvey saw no weapons on or near the bodies.[73]

The hearing was held on July 15, 16, and 18, 1861, in front of Justice of the Peace Coulter. In the end, Coulter found the charges of murder against Hickok and the others not sustained and allowed the three men to go free. He bought their argument that it was a case of self-defense. Coulter was also concerned that the county had insufficient funds to pay for the upkeep of the prisoners while they awaited trial. The accused were all employees of Russell, Majors and Waddell, the most influential corporation west of the Missouri River, and the courtroom was packed with its employees. It's interesting to note that Coulter was arrested in 1864 for embezzlement but escaped before coming to trial. The Wellmans and Doc Brink disappeared from the scene, as did James Hickok, who headed to Fort Leavenworth in Kansas, enlisting in the Union army as a civilian scout.[74]

No one really knows who shot David McCanles—Hickok or Wellman. But Wild Bill never denied it. Probably the only truthful part of Colonel George Ward Nichols's fable about Wild Bill taking on David McCanles and his gang of desperados was Hickok's statement: "I don't like to talk about that M'Kandles [sic] affair. . . . It gives me a queer shiver whenever I think of it, and sometimes I dream about it, and wake up in a cold sweat."[75]

Chapter Four

CALAMITY JANE— WILD WOMAN OF THE WEST

Just the Facts

A commotion erupted on Deadwood's Main Street. Men gawked as a cavalcade of fringed buckskin–clad outriders led by Wild Bill Hickok rode into the booming gold camp. One of these riders was Calamity Jane. The *Black Hills Pioneer*'s July 15, 1876, edition announced that "'Calamity Jane' has arrived," making no mention of Wild Bill. Within two years, she would become a national celebrity—Calamity Jane, the Wild Woman of the West.

She was born Martha Canary on May 1, 1856, on the family farm near Princeton, Missouri. Her father was Robert Willson Canary and her mother was Charlotte M. Burge, both originally from Ohio. Martha was the oldest child and had two brothers and three sisters. The young family left for the Montana goldfields in 1864. The reason for leaving may have been to escape a dispute over an inheritance from Robert's father.[1]

Along the trail, Martha perfected her horseback riding, shooting, and hunting skills. Life in Montana's goldfields was hard for the Canary family. At times, the destitute children begged for food. After Charlotte died in Blackfoot City, Montana, in the spring of 1866, Robert took the children to Salt Lake City, Utah, where he died in 1867. Little is known about how the orphaned Canary children lived. Martha claimed to have spent time at Fort Bridger, Wyoming. She turned up in Piedmont, Wyoming, in 1869. While there, she apparently worked at a variety of jobs. She lived at forts, learning how to cuss, play cards, and drink. She also frequented Cheyenne, Wyoming, and other Hell on Wheels railroad towns. By the early 1870s, Martha was going by the name Calamity Jane. In 1874, she was working at a so-called hog ranch outside Fort Laramie, Wyoming. Hog ranches sold a variety of goods, including tobacco, liquor, and female companionship.

That same year, Lieutenant Colonel George Armstrong Custer led an expedition into the Black Hills, discovering gold. In the spring of 1875, the military escorted the Newton-Jenny Expedition to confirm Custer's discovery. Calamity, disguising herself as a man, went along with the expedition until she was discovered and sent back. She returned to the Black Hills, turning up in the new boomtowns of Custer and Rapid City, Dakota Territory. In the spring of 1876, the army was tasked with finding and attacking Indian villages that had not reported to their agencies. General George Crook led two expeditions into Wyoming after the Cheyenne and Lakota. Each time, Calamity disguised herself and went along, and each time she was discovered and sent back.

In June 1876, Wild Bill Hickok's party passed through Fort Laramie on its way to Deadwood, Dakota Territory. The post commander requested that they take with them the half-naked Calamity Jane. She had been drinking with soldiers and was now locked in the guardhouse, still drunk. Wild Bill's party agreed to take her and clothed her in buckskin. Once in Deadwood, Hickok and his friends gave her money to buy female clothing. She soon repaid them with her earnings from working in dance halls.

Calamity drank hard and could tell a good tale with the best of them. People who knew her well said that she had a heart of gold. When Deadwood was struck with a smallpox outbreak, Calamity, claiming she was immune, took care of the sick.

In his 1877 book, *Black Hills Wonderland*, Horatio Maguire wrote about his first encounter with Calamity as she worked to control a bucking horse:

Throwing herself from side to side in the saddle, with the daring self-confidence of a California buchario in full career, she spurred her horse on top of the gulch, over ditches and through reservoirs and mudholes, at each leap of the fractious animal giving as good an imitation of a Sioux war-whoop as a female voice is capable of.[2]

Reading Maguire's book, the dime novelist Edward Wheeler added Calamity Jane to his popular Deadwood Dick series, bringing her national fame.

Calamity left Deadwood and the northern Black Hills by 1881, following the boom from town to town.[3] The public and newspapers followed her whereabouts and latest exploits. Excessive drinking was her downfall. She had multiple husbands and one daughter, whom she gave up. She sold photos of herself and a pamphlet about her life to make ends meet. She toured the East with a Wild West show but soon tired of that and headed back west.

Calamity returned to the Black Hills in 1903, where Dora DuFran, a Belle Fourche madam, hired her as a cook. Calamity continued to drink heavily. She died on August 1, 1903, of inflammation of the bowels and was buried in Deadwood's Mount Moriah Cemetery, near Wild Bill Hickok's grave. Calamity Jane's ever-changing legend lives on in film and print.

An Incredible Woman with an Incredible Life— Kellen Cutsforth

Over the decades and throughout the chronicling of the Old West, women have often been maligned and relegated to history's back pages. They are portrayed as either stoic wives working beside their sodbusting husbands or haggard old schoolmarms giving strict instruction in one-room schoolhouses to the children of some poor prairie farmer. Or, as often is the case, they are seen as prostitutes—soiled doves who have no family or friends and have come west due to economic hardship. They scrape together a meager existence as nothing more than human chattel passed around a miner's camp for less than the cost of a single finger of rye.

But nothing could be further from the truth. Women in the Old West were also pioneers, scouts, and Indian fighters. Perhaps no single woman during this period embodies this fact more than Martha Canary, a woman more commonly known by her nickname, Calamity Jane.

As a young girl in 1864 or 1865, around the age of eight, Calamity and her family emigrated from Missouri, taking the overland route to Virginia City, Montana, in search of gold.[4] While traveling with her family, Jane became "a remarkable good shot and a fearless rider" for a girl of her age.[5] These skills would serve her well later in life. The Canarys were destitute for much of their time in Virginia City. Sadly, Calamity's mother, Charlotte, died in 1866 in a mining camp called Blackfoot City.[6]

Following Charlotte's death, Calamity Jane's father, Robert, took Jane and her siblings to Utah.[7] The Canarys remained in Salt Lake City until 1867, when the Canary patriarch died.[8] After Robert's death, the orphaned Jane was separated from her brothers and sisters and sent to live in Wyoming Territory. These experiences, as well as her love of cigars and whiskey, molded Calamity into the hardscrabble woman with whom most people are familiar.

The great scout and buffalo hunter William F. "Buffalo Bill" Cody further corroborated Calamity's abilities at handling horseflesh as well as a shooting iron. In 1874, while employed as a guide for a military expedition led by Captain Anson Mills, Buffalo Bill wrote about meeting Calamity in Wyoming Territory's Powder River Country. He recalled Jane as a great hunter and "perfectly at home in that wild country."[9] Buffalo Bill also commented on Jane's dress, writing that when she wore men's clothing, "she might easily be mistaken for a man."[10]

The fact that Jane almost exclusively wore men's clothing and even looked and sounded like a man, due to her hard drinking and smoking, is important because this allowed her to blend in with the military officers and scouts she encountered. During this time, many historians believe that she was what is commonly referred to as a *camp follower*—that is, an individual who latched on to a military unit traveling through an area and continued to follow the unit throughout its campaign.

It is at this point that much of the controversy surrounding Calamity Jane's legacy begins to surface. Throughout her life and even after her death, Calamity Jane has been branded as a lifelong prostitute. For example, many of the reminiscences from people who claimed to have known her during her time in Montana say that she worked in a house of prostitution called the Bird Cage, where she went by the name Madame Canary. Using census sheets and numerous vital records, this attribution has been easily debunked because the facts show that Calamity would have been only eight or nine years old at the time.[11]

The fact of the matter is that very little is known about Jane's movements from 1868 to early 1875 because of the limited information in US census records.[12] After her childhood and brief mentions like that from Buffalo Bill, she really does not surface again until eventually joining the Newton-Jenney Expedition in June 1875. So any tales or information about her being a prostitute or some other solicitous character before then is pure fabrication.

In February 1876, while living near Fort Russell in Wyoming Territory, Calamity accompanied General George Crook's campaign. The area where Calamity Jane was living during this time is often referred to as a *hog ranch* or a *road ranch* and commonly associated with a prostitute's camp. This information is often used by her detractors to give little to no credence to her claims as a scout and pioneer.

In 1876, Calamity not only showed that she could survive harsh situations but also proved her worth as a real frontierswoman. During that year, General Crook and his unit confronted the great Lakota warrior Crazy Horse and a band of Sioux and Northern Cheyenne hostiles in what is today Big Horn County, Montana. This confrontation became known as the Battle of the Rosebud, which is seen by many historians as the prelude to the Battle of the Little Bighorn, the infamous battle that lead to the death of George Armstrong Custer and his entire command.

During the Rosebud battle, Crook's army took a heavy beating, and sources report that the men expended more than twenty-five thousand shells engaging the hostile Indians.[13] After suffering many casualties and significant losses, as well as exhaustion of supplies, Crook's army returned to his camp on Goose Creek. Because of the toll the battle took, many of Crook's Shoshone and Crow Indian scouts and allies abandoned him, leaving the depleted army desperate for scouts.[14]

Because of the shortage of experienced scouts, Jane served informally in this role.[15] General Crook's chief scout Frank Grouard notes in his memoirs the extreme need for scouts after the Rosebud fight and says that he hired Calamity Jane, as well as many others, to help fill the void.[16] By all accounts, she did her job well but had it cut short when she was sent away by the unit's commanding officers after they found out her sex.

Detractors of Jane's life often point to her wearing a soldier's uniform or some equivalent form of men's clothing, sneaking in with the troops, and subsequently being sent away as though her dismissal was due to her inability to perform as a scout. In fact, she was not run off because she was unable to control an ox team, scout, ride, or handle herself with a weapon. Rather, Jane was made an outcast because of the simple fact that she was a woman. If Grouard is to be believed, and he is seen by many historians as an extremely credible source, then Jane did her fair share of scouting and proved herself quite capable.

As further corroboration of her abilities, Calamity was praised by a freighter named Jesse Brown, then leading a train of twenty-five teams from Cheyenne to the Black Hills. Brown said of Calamity, when he encountered her in Wyoming Territory behind the lash of an oxen team, that "Calamity Jane was driving one of the teams, dressed in [a] buckskin suit with two Colt six shooters on a belt. She was about the roughest looking human I ever saw." He commented on her heavy-drinking lifestyle (which she also did as well as any man) by adding, "The first place that attracted her attention was a saloon, where she was soon made blind as a bat from the looking through the bottom of a glass."[17]

After her stint as a scout, Jane found herself living in Fort Laramie, Wyoming Territory, when she fell in with the famous gunfighter Wild Bill Hickok and his traveling companion Colorado Charlie Utter. Both were on their way to Dakota Territory to prospect for gold in the boomtown of Deadwood.[18] This is another greatly speculated-upon area when it comes to validating Jane's legend. Some reports say that Calamity and Wild Bill lived as husband and wife in a cabin together along Deadwood

Gulch.[19] Other sources report them as only being friends. The fact of the matter is that the true relationship between Calamity and Wild Bill may never be determined.[20]

What is indisputable, however, is that the two are buried alongside each other in Deadwood. It is hard to believe that this fact is just coincidental or that they were nothing more than old drinking buddies. It is most likely true that the two were never married (although prairie weddings, informal and often lawfully unrecognized ceremonies, were the norm during this time period), but is it so hard to believe that these two good friends could also have been lovers? Jane was certainly rough-and-tumble, having had a life full of hard drinking and hard living in an unforgiving wilderness. But does that mean a man like Wild Bill could never find affection in her arms?

What is most likely true about this infamous relationship is that these two great characters of the Old West were friends who shared an occasional tryst. Often, men and women who are friends for a while end up having more than just a friendship. In the case of Bill and Jane, these two would have been together traveling the long distance from Fort Laramie to Deadwood, sharing a lot of long and lonely nights on that well-worn trail. Whatever the case, there is no concrete evidence disproving a relationship between the two, nor any documentation proving they were anything but good friends.

With most of Jane's legend, historians and authors often take aim at her, trying to tear her apart. These same people level judgments at her for her illiteracy or her lack of cultural finesse. Those critics will then praise a frontiersman like Kit Carson for his accomplishments and in the same breath downplay his utter lack of literacy. Still other historians persist and perpetuate the myth that Jane was a lifelong prostitute, and therefore everything she ever claimed must be debunked and stricken from the historical record.

Many reminiscences, told by people who "claimed" to know Calamity, often place her in houses of prostitution or soliciting men on the street of western towns. Many of these "tales" are just that—complete and total fabrications of the truth. So the question persists: Was Calamity Jane a prostitute? And to this question I say: Who cares? Whether Calamity was a prostitute should do nothing to detract from her credibility or diminish her place in the history of the Old West. Her exploits should be given no less weight because of what she had to do to survive in an unforgiving environment that was doubly hard for a woman.

Everyone who reads material written by detractors of Jane's life should ask themselves: Are these writers on a relentless quest for the truth beyond all else? Or does the bull's-eye grow large on Calamity's back simply because she is a woman? Her life and story should be given equal weight and merit with those of any frontiersman of the time.

AN INCREDIBLE SPINNER OF TALL TALES——BILL MARKLEY

"Will the real Calamity Jane please stand up?" Just like challengers on the television show *To Tell the Truth*, it's hard to distinguish the real Calamity Jane. Today, researchers are still trying to extract gems of truth from a treasure trove of myth. The myths were ignited while Calamity was alive. She did nothing to quell their flames but stoked the blaze, attempting to live up to her own legend. Even after her death, her story continued to be embellished with false information, perpetuated to this day.

Let's start with Martha Canary's nickname: Calamity Jane. How did she come by it? She states in the book *Life and Adventures of Calamity Jane by Herself* that she was stationed with the army at a post near present-day Sheridan, Wyoming, in the early 1870s. One day, she was riding with a patrol that was suddenly ambushed by Indians. Captain Egan, commander of the post, was shot. "I . . . turned in my saddle and saw the Captain reeling in his saddle as though about to fall." Galloping back to the captain, she lifted him onto her horse in front of her and brought him back safely to the post. Egan told her, "I name you Calamity Jane, the heroine of the plains."[21]

There are problems with her account. For one thing, there is no record of Martha serving with the army as a scout or in any other capacity. Also, she did not mention the captain's first name. She may have been referring to Captain James Egan, who was stationed at Forts Sanders, Russell, and Laramie between 1868 and 1876, but there is no record that James Egan was wounded during this time or of him being rescued.[22]

Calamity Jane had H. R. Locke take her photograph in Deadwood, South Dakota, in 1889. COURTESY OF DENVER PUBLIC LIBRARY, WESTERN HISTORY COLLECTION (Z-3115)

No one else really knows why she was named Calamity Jane, although there are plenty of opinions, including that she was a good friend to know in times of calamity, she was always getting into trouble, she nursed the sick during epidemics, she created a disturbance wherever she went, her life was a disaster, and on and on. No matter how she came by the name Calamity Jane, she identified with it.

There is no evidence that she scouted for Lieutenant Colonel George Armstrong Custer or for General George Crook or for anyone else. There is no evidence to back Frank Wilstach's claim in his book *Wild Bill Hickok: Prince of Pistoleers* that in early 1876 Calamity Jane was sent to Custer with important messages from "Captain Crook." Wilstach says that Calamity almost lost her life due to the bitter cold but survived, "for otherwise she would have been with Custer in his last tragic battle on the Little Big Horn."[23] However, it's well documented that Calamity Jane disguised herself as a man and participated in the 1875 Newton-Jenny Expedition into the Black Hills until she was found out and sent back. She was also on both of Crook's expeditions against the Sioux in 1876. Multiple witnesses state that she participated dressed as a man. Both times she was discovered and sent back with returning army details.

On August 2, 1876, Jack McCall shot and killed Wild Bill Hickok in Deadwood. The night before the murder, the two men had been in a poker game together. McCall overplayed his hand, and Wild Bill called him on it. The next afternoon, Wild Bill was playing poker in Saloon Number 10 as Jack McCall walked up behind him and shot him in the head. McCall ran out into the street and attempted to mount a horse tied to the hitching rail, but the cinch had been loosened and the saddle swung under the horse's belly. As a crowd began to gather, McCall ran up the street. Calamity Jane stated, "I at once started looking for the assassin and found him at Shurdy's butcher shop and grabbed a meat cleaver and made him throw up his hands."[24]

Most likely, Jane was part of the crowd, but no one mentions whether she participated in the capture. There were so many men with guns surrounding McCall that no one wanted to shoot for fear of hitting someone else. Harry Young, who was a bartender in Saloon Number 10 and witnessed the murder, stated, "A man named Tom Mulquinn grasped him [McCall] from behind, pinned his arms while the others disarmed him."[25] The mob decided to string up McCall right then and there on a tree across from Saloon Number 10. Just in the nick of time for McCall, a Mexican rode up Main Street, grasping by the hair a severed Indian head, and distracted the mob. Cooler heads prevailed, and McCall was hustled off and locked in a log building to later stand trial.[26] The mob then joined the Mexican carting the severed head and proceeded to visit Deadwood's watering holes. Calamity Jane led the wild drunken celebration, which lasted into the next day.[27]

This incident brings us to the so-called romance between Calamity Jane and Wild Bill Hickok, which can be summarized in one word—nonsense. There is absolutely no evidence that Wild Bill and Calamity Jane had an affair. They first met when Wild Bill and his friends agreed to take Calamity Jane from the guardhouse at Fort Laramie. White Eye Anderson, who was with the Hickok party, said Calamity "laid up with Steve Utter" on the trip until they arrived in Deadwood and established their camp.[28] (Steve Utter was Colorado Charlie Utter's brother.)

Hickok had recently married the circus owner Agnes Lake, and, judging from his correspondence with her, he was in love with his wife. There are no written accounts of Wild Bill and Calamity together while in Deadwood. However, this isn't to say that they weren't friends. Wild Bill could be kind to people, and there is no doubt that he was kind to Calamity Jane. Wild Bill and his friends took her along to Deadwood, grubstaked her until she could earn her keep, and even let her imbibe from Wild Bill's private five-gallon keg of whiskey on the way to Deadwood. After Wild Bill's death and the severed-head drinking spree, Calamity must have begun the mourning process for her friend Wild Bill. Richard Hughes, who was in town at the time, said, "One sincere female mourner he [Wild Bill] did have. This was Calamity, whose grief for a time seemed uncontrollable."[29]

In his memoirs, White Eye Anderson mentions that Calamity was at Wild Bill's graveside funeral: "There were six or seven women in the procession including Calamity Jane. I remember Jane gathered some little blue flowers that grew beside the road and threw them into the grave before they filled it with sod."[30] In her reminiscences, Calamity never mentioned anything more to their relationship, referring to him as "my friend, Wild Bill."[31]

In later years, Calamity began implying that there might have been more to the relationship than just friendship; it helped her reputation to be associated with Wild Bill. In July 1903, a subtle addition was added to the romance legend. Deadwood businessman John B. Mayo found a drunken Calamity Jane sitting on a keg behind a saloon and coaxed her into having her photograph taken beside Wild Bill's grave. They climbed the steep slope to the cemetery, and as they crossed a deep ravine, Mayo remembered, "Jane was woozy, panting, and weaving as she plodded along on the high track . . . I half expected her to take a header off the trestle into the gulch bottom."[32]

The photograph Mayo took of Jane is one of the more famous ones of her in her later years. On her deathbed, it was reported that she said, "Bury me beside Wild Bill, the only man I ever loved."[33] The Deadwood townsfolk were only too happy to comply with her wishes. Having Calamity Jane buried beside Wild Bill would help with tourism. If he could, Wild Bill would have been rolling in his grave.

A breakthrough in the Calamity Jane and Wild Bill love story burst onto the national scene in 1941. On the May 6 Mother's Day episode of the radio show *We the People*, Jean Hickok McCormick announced that she was the daughter of Wild Bill Hickok and Calamity Jane. She had a diary and letters to and from Calamity and herself to prove it. Historians, writers, and film producers ran with Jean's story for fifty years without researching its authenticity. It wasn't until 1995 that Professor James D. McLaird and others showed through extensive study that the letters and diary were faked by Jean and that she was not the daughter of Wild Bill and Calamity but a fraud.[34] "I was certain before I began examining the details carefully that the 'Diary and Letters' were fraudulent," McLaird says. "Almost nothing in them coincided with the actual adventures of Calamity Jane. Besides, I was certain, after all my research, that Calamity was illiterate. It would have been impossible to have written the 'Diary and Letters' if she could neither read nor write."[35]

Another tall tale told by Calamity Jane revolved around an incident taking place on March 25, 1877, when the Cheyenne to Deadwood stagecoach was attacked outside of Deadwood. Calamity said that she was out for a ride when she saw the horses running, pulling the driverless stagecoach toward a stage station between Crook City and Deadwood, where the horses stopped. "I saw they were pursued by Indians." She looked in the stagecoach boot and saw driver Johnny Slaughter lying dead. With the Indians lurking nearby, she quickly removed all the baggage, took the driver's seat, and drove the six passengers and corpse to Deadwood.[36]

What truly occurred, however, was that five masked road agents had attempted to rob the stagecoach two and a half miles outside of Deadwood. Johnny Slaughter was shot in the heart by a shotgun blast and fell off the stagecoach into the road. The team ran for a half mile and then came to a stop. The passengers brought the stage in from there. The road agents were never caught, but there were plenty of suspicions as to who did it.[37] There is no mention of Calamity's involvement in this incident at all.

Of course, Calamity Jane did not actually do any of the things that took place in the Deadwood Dick dime novels and at times became angry when asked about them. Even though all these things are not true, there are still plenty of good Calamity Jane stories with the ring of truth. Madam Dora DuFran, who ran a brothel and gave Calamity a job as a cook, tells a story that shows Calamity's true character:

> At a turkey shoot, using a small .22 rifle, she won all the turkeys and gave them to the bystanders who hadn't had any luck. She came home without a turkey. I asked her what she had done with them, "Oh, I gave them to some poor devils who can't afford turkeys." That was Jane, always good to the underdog.[38]

Even though Calamity Jane's life was a train wreck, she lived with gusto. Though most of her reminisces were nothing more than tall tales, she must have been a great storyteller. I like Calamity Jane, and I think it would have been enjoyable to sit back and listen to her spin a yarn.

Chapter Five

DEFEAT AT THE LITTLE BIGHORN

Just the Facts

THE BATTLE OF THE LITTLE BIGHORN, AS IT IS COMMONLY KNOWN today, has also been referred to as Custer's Last Stand. The Lakota, Cheyenne, and Arapaho tribes, who were victorious on June 25 and 26, 1876, also refer to it as the Battle of the Greasy Grass. It has been said that more words have been written about the Battle of the Little Bighorn than any other battle in American history outside of Gettysburg. Truly, this one battle has become a benchmark in the American consciousness and in the history of the settling of the West.

Many authorities consider this battle, which occurred at the Little Bighorn River in eastern Montana Territory, the most prominent engagement during the Great Sioux War (1876–1877). It is remembered for the famous personalities who participated in the battle, including Sitting Bull, Crazy Horse, and Gall, and for the death of Lieutenant Colonel George Armstrong Custer and his entire immediate Seventh Cavalry command.

Custer, as a young officer, garnered a sterling Civil War record, participating in major battles such as Gettysburg and Trevilian Station. At Gettysburg, Custer led multiple mounted charges against the Confederate cavalry, helping turn the battle's tide in favor of the Union.

Following the Civil War, Custer remained in the military as a lieutenant colonel with the Seventh Cavalry, stationed in the west fighting the Indian Wars. He began to garner a reputation as a good "Indian Fighter" after scoring a victory at the Battle of Washita River in present-day Oklahoma, where he attacked a village of 250 Cheyenne Indians led by Chief Black Kettle (who perished during the battle).

Much of the conflict between the Great Plains tribes and the US military came from government lies and deceit about treaty provisions. Many Indians gave up their lands willingly but were seldom provided the annuities, agricultural supplies, schools, or anything else they had been promised. They often went to war because it was the only alternative to starving. The federal government responded with military actions forcing Indians to relocate to reservations. However, some tribes and bands continued to fight back.

In the spring of 1876, US military officials began a campaign to force the Lakota, Cheyenne, and Arapaho Indians to go to their reservations. Three separate columns of combined infantry and cavalry left their forts, converging on an area in Wyoming, Montana, and Dakota Territories believed to be inhabited by tribes considered hostile. Colonel John Gibbon's column marched east from Fort Ellis in Montana Territory, Brigadier General George Crook's column marched north toward the Powder River from Fort Fetterman in Wyoming Territory, and Brigadier General Alfred Terry's column headed west from Fort Abraham Lincoln in Dakota Territory. Terry's column included the entire twelve companies of the Seventh Calvary under the command of Lieutenant Colonel George Custer. These three columns, consisting of several thousand soldiers, were each capable of independent action but were to pursue the hostile Indian bands, destroy their resistance, and force the survivors to their reservations.

The three-pronged approach went awry, however, in mid-June when General Crook's column came to grief against a larger-than-expected force of Lakota and Cheyenne warriors at the Battle of the Rosebud, taking place along Rosebud Creek in Montana Territory. The Cheyenne and Lakota contingent was led by the great Sioux warrior Crazy Horse. The battle consisted of disconnected actions, charges, and countercharges by Crook and Crazy Horse, the two forces spread out fighting over three miles of territory. At the battle's conclusion, Crook's forces held their ground but were unable to destroy the hostile bands.

After assessing the situation, Crook realized that his troops had used up half of their ammunition supplies, and his Crow and Shoshone allies had left the battlefield for home. This decision left him without effective scouts. So Crook decided to regroup and wait for reinforcements.

Unbeknownst to Terry, Gibbon, and Custer, Crook's decision to wait for reinforcements meant that he would not converge with the other two columns when they confronted the Indians. Terry sent Custer and the Seventh Cavalry to locate and ideally trap the Indians between him and Terry and Gibbon's now-combined forces. On June 24, Custer's scouts discovered a large village of hostiles ahead of them. The following morning, Custer contemplated a surprise attack against the encampment the next day, June 26. But when he received information leading him to believe that hostile Indians had discovered their approach, he decided to attack the village immediately to prevent its inhabitants from scattering.

During the ensuing battle along the Little Bighorn River, Custer and five companies were overwhelmed in the ravines and on the hills and then engulfed by a massive combination of Indian warrior bands. The village the cavalry attacked that scorching summer day boasted between eighteen hundred and two thousand hostile combatants. It was estimated that the Seventh Cavalry lost 268 out of 700 men, including scouts and civilians. And Custer, along with 210 men under his immediate command, died that day.

RENO'S INCAPACITY AND BENTEEN'S DISOBEDIENCE— BILL MARKLEY

Could Custer and his battalion have survived the Battle of the Little Bighorn? Their only chance hinged on the actions of Major Marcus Reno and Captain Frederick Benteen. Soon after the last shots were fired, people began asking what went wrong. Brevet Captain Fredrick Whittaker, in his 1876 book, *A Popular Life of Gen. George A. Custer*, answered his own question:

Why was Custer left alone with his battalion while the other battalions were out of danger? The reasons were, Reno's incapacity and Benteen's disobedience.[1]

Major Marcus Reno, a West Point graduate, had served in the Union army during the Civil War and joined the Seventh Cavalry under Custer in 1870.[2] He became a heavy drinker after his wife died in 1874.[3] Reno took command of the Seventh Cavalry at Fort Abraham Lincoln on November 1, 1875, while Custer was on leave.[4] Custer directed Reno to ready the troops for the spring 1876 campaign, but Reno did not have the men trained to Custer's expectations upon his return to command.

The expedition left Fort Abraham Lincoln on May 17, 1876, under the overall leadership of Brigadier General Alfred Terry, with Custer in a subordinate role commanding the Seventh Cavalry. On June 10, Terry sent Reno to scout the Powder River, crossing to the Tongue River. Terry told Reno not to cross to the Rosebud River, but Reno disobeyed. Custer criticized Reno for not obtaining information on the Indians' whereabouts; Terry was upset that Reno had disobeyed orders.[5]

When Custer left on his expedition, Reno was second in command, but Custer never consulted with him and gave him no duties. During an 1879 court of inquiry, Reno was asked "whether [he] went into that fight [on the Little Bighorn] with feelings of confidence or distrust?" Reno responded,

Colonel Frederick W. Benteen. COURTESY OF DENVER PUBLIC LIBRARY, WESTERN HISTORY COLLECTION (B-296)

"I had known General Custer a long time, and I had no confidence in his ability as a soldier."[6]

Captain Frederick Benteen had served with distinction in the Union army during the Civil War. When Benteen joined the Seventh Cavalry in 1867, his first impression of Custer, his new commanding officer, was not positive.[7]

On November 27, 1868, Custer attacked a Cheyenne village along the Washita River. After capturing the village, Custer learned that many warriors were approaching his position from downriver. Major Joel Elliott and seventeen men chasing warriors in that direction had not returned. Custer sent a search party, but when the men were not found, Custer left. Weeks later, the mutilated bodies of Elliott and his men were located.

Afterward, Benteen wrote a critical letter stating that while Custer was personally shooting horses and dogs, Elliott and his men were being slaughtered. A St. Louis newspaper obtained Benteen's letter, printing it as anonymous. Custer, furious over the letter, knew that one of his staff must have written it. He called an officers meeting, announcing that he would whip whoever wrote that letter. Benteen said he did—and he was ready for the whipping. Custer said, "I'll see you again, sir!" and dismissed the officers. Custer never followed up on his threat, and Benteen saw it as unfinished business.[8]

The night of June 21, 1876, Custer and Benteen got into a heated argument. Benteen said that if there was a fight, he hoped Custer would support him better than he had supported him at Washita. Custer taunted Benteen, accusing him of killing a boy in that fight. Colonel Richard Thompson said, "It was clear Benteen hated Custer."[9]

The next morning, June 22, General Terry directed Custer to proceed up the Rosebud River, "perhaps as far as the headwaters of the Tongue, and then turn toward the Little [Big] Horn" in pursuit of Indians. Terry's column would march up the Bighorn River and position itself between the two, preventing the Indians' escape.[10]

On June 24, Custer followed a large Indian trail into the Little Bighorn watershed. The next day, June 25, scouts spotted a village fifteen miles away on the Little Bighorn River. The pack mules carrying supplies and twenty-six thousand rounds of ammunition were slowing down the column.[11] Custer assigned Captain Tom McDougall's Company B, as well as men from other companies, to escort the pack train as the rest of the Seventh Cavalry moved forward at a more rapid pace.[12]

Custer commanded the right wing, consisting of five companies; Reno commanded three companies; and Benteen commanded three companies. Custer told Benteen to reconnoiter bluffs to their left along the Little Bighorn valley and to attack any Indians he came across. If he found none, he was to quickly rejoin the main column. Custer led his battalion down the right side of today's Reno Creek, with Reno on the left.[13]

Custer's troops discovered a standing teepee holding a warrior's body. He ordered it burned. Scouts reported warriors on the run downriver. In response, Custer sent Reno a message through Lieutenant William Cooke, stating, "The Indians are about two and a half miles ahead—they are on the jump. Go forward as fast as you think proper and charge them wherever you find them and he [Custer] will support you."[14] Reno's battalion advanced at a fast trot. As Reno's men forded the Little Bighorn River, Lieutenant Charles DeRudio saw Reno drinking from a whiskey flask.[15]

While Custer's brother Boston rode back to the pack train to get a fresh mount,[16] Custer's battalion began a flanking maneuver at a fast trot along the top of the bluffs.

Reno pursued the Indians toward the village. But they were no longer running and prepared to stand and fight. Reno ordered the battalion into line of battle, then yelled, slurring, "Charge!" took a drink from his whiskey flask, and passed it to Lieutenant Benny Hodgson.[17] The battalion advanced at a gallop.

More warriors joined those Reno had been chasing. Before reaching the village, Reno halted the battalion, ordering the men to dismount and form a skirmish line. Each group of four linked their horses; three men advanced to the firing line while the fourth led the horses into the timber along the river to their right.

The Indians began flanking the skirmish line on its left. Reno ordered a withdrawal to the timber, where scout Fredric Gerard said, "I saw him [Reno] put a bottle of whisky to his mouth and drink the whole contents."[18]

Gunfire became intense. Reno decided to leave for high ground across the river. The scout Bloody Knife was shot in the head, his blood and brains splattering Reno. Flustered, Reno ordered the men to mount and then dismount three times in quick succession, then shouted, "It's all up for us boys. Follow me. It is every man for himself now."[19]

In his panic, Reno formed no rearguard; his orders were not heard by all the men, some of whom were left behind, and the wounded had to fend for themselves. Reno lost thirty-three men, most of whom were killed during his "charge" while Indians rode alongside troopers, shooting and clubbing them; many of the Indians later said it had resembled a buffalo hunt.[20]

Meanwhile, Custer saw that they were dealing with a large village. Captain Tom Custer gave Sergeant Daniel Knipe verbal orders from his brother George: "Go back to McDougall and bring him and the pack train straight across the country. Tell McDougall to hurry the pack train to Custer and if any of the packs get loose cut them and let them go unless ammunition packs; do not stop to tighten them," adding, "and if you see Benteen tell him to come on quick—a big Indian camp."[21]

After finding no Indians on his reconnaissance along the bluffs, Benteen returned to the trail, following Custer's route. The pack train was a mile behind. At an area called the morass, Benteen stopped for twenty minutes to water the horses.[22]

Boston Custer switched mounts at the pack train and trotted past Benteen's battalion. Second Lieutenant Winfield Edgerly of Company D said, "He [Boston Custer] . . . was now hurrying to join the general's immediate command. He gave me a cheery salutation as he passed and with a smile on his face rode to his death."[23] Captain Thomas Weir said to Boston, "Tell the General we are coming and will be with him shortly."[24]

An impatient Weir ordered Company D to advance without Benteen's permission. Watching Weir's company leave, Benteen ordered the rest of the battalion to follow.[25] When he reached the burning teepee, Benteen dismounted to inspect it. The men were hearing gunfire ahead.[26]

Sergeant Knipe met Benteen a mile west of the burning teepee, relaying Custer's message; then he rode to the pack train now at the teepee and gave Custer's message to McDougall.[27] Although he knew Custer wanted him to come quick, Benteen only proceeded at a fast walk.[28]

Meanwhile, at Custer's battalion, Custer told Cooke to send Benteen a message. Cooke assigned this task to his orderly Giovanni Martini. Cooke wrote:

> *Benteen*
> *Come on*
> *Big Village*
> *Be quick*
> *Bring packs.*
> *[signed by W. W. Cooke]*
> *P.S. bring pacs [sic].*[29]

Martini encountered Boston Custer along the trail before galloping up to Benteen with Custer's order. Benteen said the message was confusing. How could he hurry and bring the packs too? He sent Martini to the pack train to hurry it up and ordered his battalion forward as the sound of gunfire increased. Seeing Reno's men on the bluffs, they rode toward them. Reno rode out, shouting, "For God's sake, Benteen, halt your command and help me."[30] Private William Morris of Company M, part of Reno's battalion, wrote, "Benteen . . . came up as slow as though going to a funeral. . . . He was simply in no hurry; and Muller . . . told me they walked all the way, and they heard heavy firing while they were watering their horses."[31]

Reno and Benteen remained on the bluff, ignoring Custer's messages. Officers and troopers heard heavy volleys of gunfire coming from downriver, but Reno and Benteen later denied hearing anything.[32] Most of the Indians raced toward the sound of the gunfire.

Hearing continued heavy gunfire from Custer's direction during the long period of inaction, Weir and Edgerly agreed that they needed to go to Custer. Edgerly watched Weir talk to Benteen and Reno, mount his horse, and ride toward the gunfire. Edgerly ordered Company D to follow. He later learned that Reno had refused to give Weir permission, so Weir left on his own.[33]

Reaching Reno's position with the pack train, McDougall saw no skirmish line, so he quickly ordered his men to form one.[34]

A half hour after Weir left, Reno and Benteen decided to follow.[35] The troops advanced to what is now Weir Point and halted as the Indians came racing toward them. The battalions retreated to Reno's original position, where they made their stand that day and into the next. Captain Benteen unofficially took command from Major Reno.[36] Terry and his column arrived two days later, discovering the bodies of Custer and his men.

Was Reno drunk? Yes. Eyewitnesses attested to his drinking, slurring, and odd behavior. Reno confided to his longtime friend Rev. Dr. Arthur Edwards that he was drunk at the Little Bighorn.[37] Lieutenant Edward Godfrey, who was with Benteen, wrote, "Frankly, I do not believe Custer's command would have been rescued under Reno's leadership. At no time during the battle was his conduct such as to inspire confidence."[38]

Could Benteen have reached Custer in time? Yes. Benteen had disobeyed a direct order from his commanding officer to come quick. Richard Roberts, Custer's private secretary, wrote,

He [Reno] could have reached Custer, for Boston Custer came back and got a drink of water from one of Company K's men who were with Benteen, under Captain Godfrey. I know this, for one of the wounded soldiers told me so. . . . Boston Custer got back, and was found dead near his brother the General.[39]

In June 1878, General Nelson A. Miles visited the battlefield, writing,

The distance from where the running Reno halted and kept the seven troops and the reserve ammunition [Reno-Benteen siege site], to the extreme right of Custer's command [Last Stand Hill] was about four miles. A cavalry horse walked that distance in fifty-eight minutes. At a smart trot or gallop, as a cavalryman goes into action, fifteen minutes would have brought the whole command [Reno, Benteen, and packs] into the engagement and the result might have been entirely different. This we proved on that same ground by the actual test of moving our horses over it, and timing them by the watch.[40]

In June 2013, National Park Service seasonal ranger Michael Donahue and Little Bighorn historian George Kush conducted time and motion studies. "We used experienced horsemen dressed in period attire, with correct arms and equipment," Kush said.

> *We concluded it takes under eight minutes to ride at a steady lope, or as Trumpeter Martini put it, "on the jump" from the Reno-Benteen siege site boundary to Custer's battlefield. Due to National Park Service restrictions, we could not start at the Reno-Benteen monument proper, but at the fence line and met the same requirements upon reaching Custer's battlefield. However, we concluded General Miles statement, "that fifteen minutes would have brought the whole command into the engagement" to be absolutely correct.[41]*

If Reno had not been drunk, and if Benteen had obeyed orders, Custer and his men might have survived the Battle of the Little Bighorn.

CUSTER'S BRAVADO—KELLEN CUTSFORTH

When it comes to the likes of George Armstrong Custer, there is perhaps no name better known for utter disaster in Western history or the conflicts known as the Indian Wars. As Dale L. Walker succinctly puts it, the name Custer has become synonymous "with the worst debacle in American military annals."[42] On June 25 and 26, 1876, George Custer blundered into infamy and the history books in what is seen by many as a totally avoidable destruction of his immediate Seventh Cavalry command.

Before his infamous death, however, Custer demonstrated an out-of-control ego, bravado, and lack of good judgment, which would eventually contribute to his undoing. When he was a student at West Point, Custer received numerous demerits for mostly minor infractions. But many felt that his constant troublemaking showed he had little respect for rules or for the army itself.[43]

As an example of his disregard for proper procedure, Custer received a court-martial twice in six years.[44] For his first court-martial, he was charged with "Neglect of Duty," and in the subsequent trial, he was found guilty on all charges, but the court was lenient and did not sentence him to anything harsher than a "reprimand in orders."[45] Perhaps it was the outcome of this court-martial that set Custer up to have an overinflated ego and the belief that he could not be touched, that he could get away with anything.

No matter the trial's outcome, Custer's career continued. He would go on to serve in the Civil War under Generals Irwin McDowell, George B. McClellan, and Alfred Pleasonton. At the age of twenty-three, Custer was the youngest soldier in the Union army to receive a promotion to brigadier general of volunteers.[46] As a commander and soldier, Custer was fearless in battle. During the Civil War, and most notably the Battle of Gettysburg, he led nearly forty men in a mounted charge against a Confederate line. This action resulted in twenty-seven men captured, dead, or suffering wounds and Custer himself having his horse shot out from under him. After the charge, he returned to the Union lines with only thirteen men unscathed.[47]

On the third day of the same battle, Custer's superior, General David Gregg, disobeyed a direct order and ordered Custer to remain with the brigade. The Confederates, armed with 150 artillery pieces, began the largest Southern bombardment of the war. For two hours, the Confederates fired upon the main Union line. The Confederate forces were using this attack to prepare the way for an assault by twelve thousand men led by Major General George Pickett.[48]

Lieutenant Colonel George Armstrong Custer. Photograph taken by David Francis Barry in New York City, March 1876. COURTESY OF DENVER PUBLIC LIBRARY, WESTERN HISTORY COLLECTION (B-56)

Three miles away, General Robert E. Lee instructed his most admired cavalry officer, General J. E. B. Stuart, to swing around the Union flank and destroy the enemy.[49] The only force standing in Stuart's way was the Michigan Brigade, with General Custer in command. With saber drawn, decked out in a black velvet uniform, Custer led his mounted men in a charge against the mobilized Confederate cavalry. Although badly outnumbered, Custer urged his cavalry on into a furious battle. Again, his horse was shot out from under him, but, as before, he survived, and his charge allowed Union troops to drive into the rebels' formation and split it apart, turning the fight into a Confederate rout.[50]

These incidents have become great examples of what is now commonly referred to as "Custer's luck." His good fortune in battle, as in other aspects of his life, more than likely contributed to his military failure at the Battle of the Little Bighorn. His ego and overconfidence cannot be overstated when it comes to his style of commanding in the field.

After the Civil War, Custer mustered out of volunteer service on February 1, 1866. After mustering out, he explored several options of employment, including careers in railroads and mining, and he even did some investing in New York City. But these career paths did not pan out.[51] So on July 28, 1866, Custer received an appointment to the rank of lieutenant colonel in the Seventh Cavalry.[52] This lowering of rank was a common practice, with many men reverting to their actual ranks after serving in much higher brevet capacity during the Civil War.

After receiving his new assignment, Custer entered the Plains Indian Wars. In 1868, he claimed victory in what is referred to as the Battle of Washita in Oklahoma Territory. This victory would earn Custer a reputation as a great Indian fighter, further boosting his ego and his belief in his own invincibility. During the battle, Custer employed a strategic tactic that would ultimately lead to his demise at the Battle of the Little Bighorn.

The Washita battle unfolded with Custer leading a charge from the north into the snow-drenched village in the heart of winter. It was reported that "the regiment galloped through the tepees from several directions, firing indiscriminately and killing men and women alike."[53] Caught by total surprise, the Cheyenne village was unable to respond to Custer's onslaught, and the battle ended in a total rout in about ten minutes.[54]

Little did Custer realize, however, that the village he had just destroyed was only a small outcropping of the enemy's actual extent. Lieutenant Edward S. Godfrey, who was riding with the cavalry that day, was in pursuit of some stray ponies when he discovered tepees "as far as I could see down the well wooded, tortuous valley. . . . Not only could I see tepees, but mounted warriors scurrying in our direction."[55]

Estimates say there were possibly thousands of hostile Indians plotting Custer's destruction; only through an ingenious feint, in which Custer fooled the Indians into believing that he was mounting an attack, were he and his regiment able to slink away.[56] Had he employed proper reconnaissance, Custer would have known of the imminent threat and perhaps not been so hasty to attack Chief Black Kettle's Cheyenne band. Either way, on Custer's return to Camp Supply in Oklahoma Territory, he was greeted with much pageantry and as a conquering hero. Word spread quickly of his "success," and much of the western press praised his Indian fighting prowess.[57] Ironically, had it not been for the vaunted "Custer's luck," George Custer's golden scalp may very well have been dangling from a horse bridle or made into a Cheyenne war shirt that day.

Nearly ten years after his "victory" at the Washita, Custer testified before congressional committees against President Ulysses S. Grant's administration over fraud in the Bureau of Indian Affairs. After being forced to remain in Washington as his regiment headed for hostile Sioux country, Custer sent a letter to Grant, pleading, "I appeal to you as a soldier to spare me the humiliation of seeing my regiment march to meet the enemy & I do not share its dangers."[58] After pressure from some of Custer's allies in the military, Grant relented and allowed Custer to rejoin the Seventh Cavalry on the condition that General Alfred Terry, not Custer, command the expedition.

As the summer campaign of 1876 got into full swing, Custer left Fort Abraham Lincoln in Dakota Territory. Preparing to head out on the trail of hostile Indians, General Terry offered Custer the use of an additional battalion of Second Cavalry, as well as a Gatling gun battery—these guns could discharge 350 rounds a minute and were often quite useful in combat. Custer refused both offers.[59]

Custer's reasons for refusing the Gatling gun battery lay in the fact that he felt the weapons would slow down his advance. They were large, cumbersome guns that often jammed and had to be pulled by as many as four horses and frequently had to be moved by hand when navigating around objects in the field. Whether they would have saved Custer and his command at the Little Bighorn is debatable. The refusal of Second Cavalry troops, however, was pure ego on Custer's part. As to the refusal of more troops, he was quoted as saying, "[The Seventh Cavalry] could handle anything."[60] He sacrificed manpower to be able to move quickly and engage the enemy. His decision to do so was a tactical error, to put it mildly.

Then, as his forces approached the combined Sioux, Cheyenne, and Arapaho village in Montana Territory, Custer repeated the same mistake he had made during the Washita battle. He did not gather adequate reconnaissance of the humongous hostile village he was about to engage. He instead inexplicably split his twelve companies into four battalions. One was led by Major Marcus Reno, which included three companies. Another three companies were led by Captain Frederick Benteen, while five companies fell under Custer's command, and the final battalion (composed of the twelfth company plus six men from each of the other companies) was assigned to guard the pack train of supplies.[61]

Custer and Reno separated from Benteen, who scouted to their left and was instructed that if he found no Indians, he was to return quickly to the main column, while Reno and Custer would surround and attack the village from the sides.[62] Custer planned to attack the Sioux just as he had the Cheyenne village on the Washita nearly ten years earlier, by surprising his foe, scattering them, and turning the battle into a rout. He believed "Custer's luck" would not run dry and he would easily secure the victory because he had little respect for the Indians' fighting skills.

Unfortunately for Custer and his command, his calculations were incorrect. The information gleaned by his scouts as to the enormity of what lay before them was not given proper consideration. In fact, four Crow Indian scouts and scout Mitch Boyer informed the commander of the village's size, saying, "General, I have been with these Indians for 30 years, and this is the largest village I have ever heard of."[63]

As further proof of Custer's denial of the monstrous village, First Lieutenant Charles DeRudio rode out with Custer on the morning of the battle in response to the reports Custer received from the scouts and noted, "In the morning of 6/25 Custer had been up ahead with the scouts and with his [field] glasses. He said [the field glasses] were not strong enough to discover anything."[64] This was the extent of Custer's reconnaissance. He did not see what his scouts were telling him; therefore, it was of no consequence to him.

Splitting his forces, not doing proper surveillance, and then charging headlong into a massive enemy force are the reasons for the military debacle at the Little Bighorn. And these decisions were made by Custer and Custer alone. The results of this most famous battle did not hinge on a drunken Marcus Reno or the slow response of Captain Frederick Benteen. Defeat and death were secured when Custer ignored the reports of his scouts and then split his force in the face of an overwhelming enemy.

Reno's drunkenness certainly did not help matters, but when he was confronted by the sheer volume of hostile combatants residing in the combined Sioux, Cheyenne, and Arapaho village, Reno found himself and his command completely outnumbered, outflanked, and outgunned. There was no chance of victory, let alone any chance to save Custer and his men. Reno and Benteen barely survived, fighting off an onslaught of Indians determined to wipe them out as they held their ground from a makeshift defensive position.

The facts in this matter are clear: George Armstrong Custer made numerous egregious errors that led to the deaths of nearly three hundred men. He believed "Custer's luck" made him impervious to destruction. And Custer thought that if he remained at the battalion's helm, his men could whip any enemy they encountered. In reality, he was dead wrong.

Chapter Six

THE REALITY OF BUFFALO BILL CODY

Just the Facts

WILLIAM FREDERICK "BUFFALO BILL" CODY WAS BORN ON FEBRUARY 26, 1846, in LeClaire, Iowa. He was the son of Isaac Cody, a farmer who was also a staunch abolitionist. In 1853, Bill's father sold their farm in Iowa and moved his family to Fort Leavenworth, Kansas Territory. While there, Isaac railed against the evils of slavery, and while speaking at a trading post where proslavery men often gathered, he was stabbed with a bowie knife by a man who disagreed with his opinion.

Though Isaac survived this attempt on his life, he never fully recovered from the injuries and died in 1857 from a respiratory infection compounded by the lingering effects of the stabbing. After the death of the Cody patriarch, the family suffered financially. This forced Bill, being too young for military service at the tender age of eleven, to take a job with a freight carrier, riding up and down the length of a wagon train delivering messages between the drivers and workmen.

In 1863, at the age of seventeen, Bill joined the US Army as a teamster with the rank of private. He later served in Company H of the Seventh Kansas Volunteer Cavalry until he was honorably discharged in 1865. The following year, Cody married Louisa Frederici, and the couple eventually had four children. In 1868, Cody worked as a civilian chief of scouts for the Fifth US Cavalry. In this role, Bill served during the Plains Indian Wars, participating in sixteen battles.

When he was not scouting and tracking Indians for the military, Bill hunted buffalo, which provided food for the army and for the workers on the Kansas Pacific Railroad. It was his prowess with a rifle and hunting buffalo that eventually earned Cody the nickname Buffalo Bill. In 1869, Cody was introduced to Edward Carroll Zane Judson, an author who went by the pen name Ned Buntline. Impressed by the young man, Buntline published a novel under the title *Buffalo Bill, King of the Bordermen*, which afforded Cody a great deal of national celebrity and helped make Buffalo Bill a household name.

Because of the popularity of Buntline's novel, many other authors wrote similar stories in dime novels and nickel weeklies, further popularizing Bill's name and exploits in the Old West. In 1872, Buffalo Bill made his stage-acting debut in Chicago in a play produced by Ned Buntline called *The Scouts of the Prairie*. It was a smash, playing to sellout crowds.

As Bill found fame with these productions, he also toured with his own acting troupe, called the Buffalo Bill Combination. During the acting season's downtime, he continued to scout on the Great Plains. Eventually, in 1883 near North Platte, Nebraska, Buffalo Bill created Buffalo Bill's Wild West. This enterprise was a large entertainment spectacle that brought scenes and stories of the Old West to the national populace.

The show included displays of sharpshooting expertise, elements of the rodeo, traditional dance performances by Indians, and reenactments of historic events that took place in the Old West. Some of the more popular reenactments included the riding of the Pony Express, Indian attacks on wagon trains, stagecoach robberies, and the Battle of the Little Bighorn, also known as Custer's Last Stand. In this production, Buffalo Bill often portrayed General George Armstrong Custer valiantly perishing at the climax of the battle.

Cody, however, found his greatest success in 1887, when he and his Wild West troupe ventured overseas to Great Britain and performed for Queen Victoria and other dignitaries inside packed houses and stadiums. This popularity followed Bill on his return trip home to the United States, and he became one of the most popular and recognizable people in the entire country, if not the world.

Along with his newfound fame, Buffalo Bill became extremely wealthy. Capitalizing on his fortune, Bill purchased a large amount of ranchland in North Platte and invested in numerous business ventures. Unfortunately for Bill, many of these ventures did not pan out. These failures, accompanied by his continued lending of money to friends and acquaintances with no hope of seeing repayment, caused Bill and his family to experience numerous financial wobbles.

These economic troubles eventually led Buffalo Bill to sell off most of his ranchland in North Platte and combine interests with one of his Wild West show competitors, a man named Gordon William Lillie, who went by the stage name Pawnee Bill. This combined enterprise was known as the Two Bills show. This business would eventually be foreclosed on, and Buffalo Bill would spend his remaining days working for the Sells-Floto Circus until his death in 1917.

As Big as the West——Kellen Cutsforth

Historian and executive director of the Buffalo Bill Museum and Grave in Golden, Colorado, Steve Friesen once said, "If Buffalo Bill did even half of what he said he did then he is one of, if not the greatest frontiersman the West has ever known." So just how much of what William Frederick "Buffalo Bill" Cody said really was true? To answer this question, it is best to begin by examining his life on the Great Plains as a young man.

In his autobiography, Buffalo Bill claimed that, as a fifteen-year-old boy, he had ridden for the Pony Express. The Pony Express was a service delivering messages, newspapers, and mail across the country via horseback. It was founded by William H. Russell, Alexander Majors, and William B. Waddell, all of whom were notable in the freighting business.[1] The enterprise ran for just nineteen months, from April 3, 1860, to October 1861, when it was eventually replaced by the telegraph system. Although this mail service existed for an extremely short time, it has been well remembered and romanticized through novels, histories, video games, and motion pictures. It is one Old West enterprise that continues to receive a great deal of public interest.

Buffalo Bill Cody in 1889, Paris, France.
COURTESY OF DENVER PUBLIC LIBRARY,
WESTERN HISTORY COLLECTION (NS-226)

Detractors of Bill's legacy often point to his claims of riding for the Pony Express as symbolic of creating his own legacy. Many of the discrepancies with Bill's claim of riding for the Pony Express come from contradictory information about dates and his activities.[2] It is a fact, however, that Cody did work for the parent company of the Pony Express: Russell, Majors and Waddell. And in his memoir, *Seventy Years on the Frontier*, Alexander Majors backed Bill's claims, writing that Cody was indeed part of the Pony Express.[3]

Critics of Buffalo Bill also suggest that he invented working for the Pony Express to add to his reputation as a fearless frontiersman. But one could respond to these critiques, as historian Steve Friesen has suggested, by asking: Did Buffalo Bill become famous because of the Pony Express? Or did the Pony Express become famous because of Buffalo Bill? The Pony Express was featured in Buffalo Bill's Wild West for almost thirty years, gaining immense popularity. Prior to that, it was little more than a historical footnote.[4]

Following his time with the Pony Express, Cody worked as a buffalo hunter for the Kansas Pacific Railroad, providing meat for the workers from 1867 to 1872. During this period, he received the nickname he would be associated with for the rest of his life, "Buffalo Bill." Reminiscing about his work, Cody wrote, "As soon as one buffalo would fall, Brigham [his horse] would take me so close to the next, that I could almost touch it with my gun."[5] On buffalo hunts, Bill became so lethal with his 1866 Springfield rifle that he eventually nicknamed it Lucretia Borgia after the most famous member of the ruthless Italian Borgia family.

While working for the Kansas Pacific Railroad, Cody and another man named Bill Comstock became two of the most well-known buffalo hunters in the area. This led many of the railroaders to start calling both men "Buffalo Bill." So, to claim ownership of the nickname, both Bills competed in a contest to see who could kill the most buffalo in a single hunt. The contest took place near the town of present-day Oakley, Kansas, and was presided over by several referees. By late afternoon on the day of the hunt, Cody had killed sixty-nine buffalo while Comstock had killed only forty-six. After Cody was declared "champion buffalo hunter of the Plains," he was forever known by the nickname Buffalo Bill. It is true that there are no newspaper articles corroborating this story, but anecdotal data, as well as strong archaeological evidence, back Cody's account.[6]

Over seventeen months working for the railroad, Cody killed 4,280 buffalo. Along with debate over his nickname, this portion of Bill's life is a source of contention. Many conservationists say that he played a significant role in the mass slaughter of the buffalo on the Great Plains. But when the Kansas Pacific Railroad was completed, Buffalo Bill curtailed most of his hunting. In truth, his 4,280 total is quite miniscule in comparison to the millions of buffalo living on the Great Plains. And the near extinction of the buffalo happened a decade after Bill's most active years.[7] Later in life, Cody spoke out against hide hunting and advocated the establishment of a hunting season.[8]

While earning a living as a buffalo hunter, Cody also scouted for the army during the Indian Wars. What is even more extraordinary is that between 1868 and 1869 Bill saw action in at least nine separate battles.[9] The most daunting battle that Bill participated in was the Battle of Summit Springs, which took place in northeastern Colorado. Leading up to this battle, a group of Cheyenne Dog Soldiers led by a warrior named Tall Bull were raiding settlements throughout Kansas and Nebraska. The attacks by the Cheyenne in these areas resulted in the murder of many defenseless settlers and the kidnapping of two white women, including Susanna Alderdice.[10]

Acting as a guide, Buffalo Bill led 244 soldiers of the US Fifth Cavalry and 50 Pawnee scouts to the Dog Soldier village, containing

500 inhabitants, near Summit Springs.[11] On July 11, 1869, the cavalry attacked the village, killing nearly fifty warriors and saving one of the female captives. Unfortunately, they were unable to save Susanna Alderdice, who was murdered as the attack commenced.[12] During the fight, Buffalo Bill was credited with gunning down Tall Bull as he attempted to escape from the battle.[13]

In the following three years after Summit Springs, Cody saw action in several other battles. On April 26, 1872, Bill was involved in an engagement, although not as dramatic as Summit Springs, where his actions were deemed valorous and worthy of recognition by the officers with whom he served. After he was recommended for commendation, Buffalo Bill received the Medal of Honor on May 22, 1872.[14]

For some historians, the waters become muddied concerning Bill's life and legacy around this time. In 1869, the same period in which Buffalo Bill was battling Cheyenne Dog Soldiers, Ned Buntline's novel *Buffalo Bill, King of the Bordermen* was first serialized in the pages of the *Chicago Tribune*. So while Bill was fighting Indians on the Great Plains and winning a Medal of Honor for valor, he was also being lionized within the pages of popular literature.

To further compound the confusion between his actual life and the myth of his legend, Buffalo Bill made his stage-acting debut in 1872. He took the stage alongside his good friend and fellow frontiersman Texas Jack Omohundro. In the following years, he would also appear in stage plays about life on the Great Plains with his good friend and known gunfighter James Butler "Wild Bill" Hickok. These performances contained embellishments for greater entertainment value. It is here that many take aim at the obvious fabrications in dime novels and stage productions and hypothesize that if these stories are lies, then everything Buffalo Bill ever said must be a lie, which could not be further from the truth.

Following his success as a stage actor, and seeing profit in the venture, Cody built the business that ultimately became his legacy: Buffalo Bill's Wild West. Debuting in 1883, this outdoor attraction took a few years to find a foothold in the country's burgeoning entertainment industry. After experiencing several financial wobbles in the enterprise's infancy, Bill found great success in early 1887.

In March of that same year, Buffalo Bill took his entire troupe overseas to England, where his Wild West took part in an event known as the American Exhibition.[15] This exposition featured displays of the latest agricultural, mechanical, and textile products and inventions from all around the United States, but the main attraction was Buffalo Bill's Wild West.[16] Bill performed for numerous dignitaries and was so successful that many reports state that Bill received a standing salute from Queen Victoria herself.[17]

Upon returning to the United States, the great fanfare Cody had experienced in England followed him home. In short order, Buffalo Bill became the most recognized American in the world and the most requested guest of British royalty.[18] This success and fame helped Bill amass a large fortune that was equaled by very few in the country.

Many historians looking to downplay Buffalo Bill's accomplishments as a businessman often turn a jaundiced eye toward his employment of Indians in his show. These critics normally accuse Cody of abusing the native peoples and taking advantage of them. There is absolutely no truth to these accusations whatsoever. In fact, throughout Cody's tenure as a showman, the Indians he employed received good pay, had an opportunity to leave the reservation, and could share their culture with the rest of the world. He also frequently referred to them as "the Americans" as a sign of respect.[19]

Buffalo Bill believed that these opportunities were a great chance for many Indians to improve their lives. He respected them and usually described them as "the former foe, present friend, the American," and he once said that "every Indian outbreak that I have ever known has resulted from broken promises and broken treaties by the government."[20] The great Sioux chief Sitting Bull, whom Buffalo Bill employed in his show, had great respect for Cody and counted him as a friend.[21]

During his life, Cody also supported the rights of women. He was quoted as saying, "What we want to do is give women even more liberty than they have. Let them do any kind of work they see fit, and if they do it as well as men, give them the same pay."[22] As a sign that he practiced what he preached, the most famous performer in his show, Annie Oakley, was a woman.

Buffalo Bill Cody stands in front of the Deadwood Stage. John Y. Nelson, scout and driver of the coach, sits on top. COURTESY OF DENVER PUBLIC LIBRARY, WESTERN HISTORY COLLECTION (NS-15)

Bill's early stage performances, being featured in highly embellished fiction, and spending his later life as a showman unfortunately hurt his legacy. Cody's time in the entertainment industry caused many detractors and debunkers to pick at his life like buzzards scavenging on a buffalo carcass.

In truth, Buffalo Bill was a Pony Express rider, frontiersman, prospector, Civil War soldier, Indian fighter, scout, and buffalo hunter.[23] He eventually became the most famous American of his day and rich beyond compare. His claims are anchored by indisputable facts and a multitude of primary resources. Simply put, William "Buffalo Bill" Cody lived an amazing life and may very well be the greatest historical figure in the annals of the American West.

BUFFALO BILL CODY AND HIS MYTHIC WEST——BILL MARKLEY

"One day as I was leaving Horse Creek, a party of fifteen Indians jammed me in a sand ravine eight miles west of the station. They fired at me repeatedly, but my luck held and I went unscathed," stated William F. Cody in his autobiography. Cody, carrying mail for the Pony Express, dug his spurs into his horse's sides and outran his pursuers. After being chased eleven miles to Sweetwater Bridge Station, Cody found that Indians had killed the stock tender and stolen the horses. He continued for another twelve miles, reaching Plonts Station, where he obtained a fresh mount and rode to the next station.[24] What a great story. Unfortunately, the only record of this incident is in Cody's book.

Buffalo Bill is one of my heroes, but come with me where many may fear to venture. William F. Cody embellished facts. Let's start with his autobiography. Many historians consider it fiction, belonging on the shelves alongside the dime novels that made Buffalo Bill famous. First published in 1879, his autobiography was revised several times with the help of ghostwriters. The first edition is considered the most accurate.

Some historians believe that Cody never rode for the Pony Express. He did work for the freighting company Russell, Majors and Waddell, carrying dispatches to and from its freighting outfits, herding livestock, and driving wagons as far as Salt Lake City.[25] Russell, Majors and Waddell later established the Pony Express, but there are no records of who was employed as riders. Three witnesses stated that Cody rode for the Pony Express. Two are dubious, coming forward years after Cody was famous; the third, Alexander Majors of Russell, Majors and Waddell, is respectable, but a Cody ghostwriter helped him write his memoirs and Cody grubstaked the writing.[26] Cody's sister Julia wrote that during the run of the Pony Express, she and Cody attended school in Leavenworth, Kansas, taught by Valentine Devinny, who was there between the fall of 1860 and sometime in 1862. Devinny remembered Cody attending his school and that he was "a determined ball player."[27]

Cody made many unsubstantiated claims. He said he was in the 1857–1858 Mormon War. While alone in a cabin, he met Chief Rain-in-the-Face, who some later thought killed Lieutenant Colonel George Custer. Cody joined Wild Bill Hickok and others in attacking an Indian village on the Powder River in Wyoming and retrieving stolen horses. However, none of these stories can be verified.

With the outbreak of the Civil War, Cody joined antislavery Kansas Jayhawkers attacking proslavery neighbors. Cody believed the knife attack on his father by a slavery supporter had led to his father's death, and he was out for revenge. His mother made him quit. But in the summer of 1862, Cody joined the antislavery guerrillas known as Red Legs. They killed proslavery sympathizers, burned homes, destroyed crops, and stole livestock. Cody glossed over his involvement with the Red Legs, saying they chased after proslavery Bushwhackers such as William Quantrill and the James and Younger brothers. In 1863, the Ninth Kansas Volunteers hired Cody as a civilian scout. After spending a night carousing in Leavenworth, Cody awoke the morning of February 19, 1864, and found that he had enlisted in the Seventh Kansas Volunteer Cavalry, where he remained for the duration of the war.

Cody was good friends with Wild Bill Hickok. He idolized Hickok to the extent that he tried to appear to be the same as Hickok and included himself in many of Hickok's tales. People confused Cody with Hickock, and Cody never corrected the confusion. During his Wild West performances in London, Cody requested General William T. Sherman's endorsement. Sherman wrote that Cody "guided me honestly and faithfully in 1865–66 from Fort Riley to Kearny in Kansas and Nebraska." The only problem with this glowing endorsement? It was Hickok who guided Sherman, not Cody. Cody never corrected the error but went on to use Sherman's statement in his promotions.[28]

Cody tried various occupations, settling on buffalo hunting to provide meat for Kansas Pacific Railroad workers. Because of this, some critics link him with the bison near extinction. Cody also began scouting for the army in 1868, and on July 11, 1869, he participated in Lieutenant Colonel Eugene Carr's Fifth Cavalry attack on the Cheyenne Dog Soldier village at Summit Springs, Colorado. Cody claimed to have killed the Dog Soldiers' leader, Tall Bull. He stated that after seeing a Cheyenne leader encouraging his men from atop of a large bay horse, he was determined to have the horse and shot the leader out of the saddle.[29]

According to Cody, after the fight a woman saw him with the horse and began crying. He learned that she was a wife of Tall Bull. She told Cody that it was Tall Bull's favorite warhorse and she had last seen Tall Bull riding it. Cody told her Tall Bull would never ride the horse again. "I informed her henceforth I should call the gallant steed 'Tall Bull,' in honor of her husband."[30] But other participants, including one of Tall Bull's wives interviewed by Carr, claimed that Tall Bull had fought and died on foot. Many times, Cheyenne Dog Soldiers fought on foot to the death, tethering themselves to leather straps staked to the ground. Luther North claimed that his brother Frank had killed Tall Bull, while a Cheyenne painting depicts Pawnee scouts shooting Tall Bull as he fought on foot in a ravine.[31] Nevertheless, Cody's version of killing Tall Bull was reenacted in his Wild West production years later.

An 1876 skirmish later became a popular Wild West reenactment. The government ordered all tribes to report to their reservations by January 31, 1876, and remain there or be considered hostile. That spring, three major armies converged on "hostile" tribes in Wyoming, Montana, and Dakota Territories.

Cody, learning that the armies were on the march, ended his theatrical performance and, bringing along his stage outfit, hustled west to join Lieutenant Colonel Carr and his Fifth Cavalry comrades at Fort Laramie. The Fifth Cavalry was ordered to join General George Crook's army in northern Wyoming. They left Fort Laramie on June 22. Reaching the Cheyenne River, they encamped until July 3, waiting for supplies. Colonel Wesley Merritt took over command from Carr on July 1, and on July 7 news reached camp that Custer and approximately 268 men had been killed at the Little Bighorn. On July 13, Merritt received news that many Cheyenne were leaving Red Cloud Agency and the Fifth Cavalry was to intercept them. On the evening of July 16, the Fifth Cavalry made camp on Warbonnet Creek in Nebraska.

The next morning, they sighted a scouting party of Cheyenne warriors from Morning Star's Northern Cheyenne band.[32] One of these warriors was named Yellow Hair because of a blond woman's scalp that he carried.[33]

Cody, dressed in his theatrical attire, sat astride his horse alongside the officers on top of a ridge. The Cheyenne did not see the Fifth Cavalry, but they did see the Fifth Cavalry's supply train advancing toward them as two couriers rode in advance of the column to find the Fifth. A dozen warriors rode to intercept the men. The order was given for Cody and other scouts, along with a dozen men from Company K, to attack the Cheyenne. Of the attack, Cody wrote:

> [T]he Indians . . . suddenly turned upon us. . . . One of the Indians, who was handsomely decorated with all the ornaments usually worn by a war chief when engaged in a fight, sang out to me, in his own tongue:
>
> "I know you, Pa-he-haska; if you want to fight, come ahead and fight me."
>
> The chief was riding his horse back and forth in front of his men, as if to banter me, and I concluded to accept the challenge. I galloped towards him for fifty yards and he advanced towards me about the same distance, both of us riding at full speed, and then, when we were only about thirty yards apart, I raised my rifle and fired; his horse fell to the ground, having been killed by my bullet.
>
> Almost at the same instant my own horse went down, he having stepped into a hole. The fall did not hurt me much, and I instantly sprang to my feet. The Indian had also recovered himself, and we were

*now both on foot, and not more than twenty paces apart. We fired at
each other simultaneously. My usual luck did not desert me on this
occasion, for his bullet missed me, while mine struck him in the breast.
He reeled and fell, but before he had fairly touched the ground I was
upon him, knife in hand, and had driven the keen-edged weapon to
its hilt in his heart. Jerking his war-bonnet off, I scientifically scalped
him in about five seconds. . . .*

*[T]he Indians . . . came charging down upon me from a hill, in
hopes of cutting me off. General Merritt . . . ordered . . . Company K
to hurry to my rescue.*

*The order came none too soon, for had it been given one minute
later I would have had not less than two hundred Indians upon me.
As the soldiers came up I swung the Indian chieftain's top-knot and
bonnet in the air, and shouted: "The first scalp for Custer."*[34]

Cody left the army on August 22, 1876, before the campaign's
end, explaining that he had theatrical commitments; however, he had
none.[35] He soon was acting in his new play *Red Right Hand; or, Buffalo
Bill's First Scalp for Custer.* The action was hand-to-hand combat, and
dialogue with Cody's Cheyenne foe was added. Instead of Yellow Hair,
the fallen Cheyenne's name was mistranslated Yellow Hand, and it was
never corrected.

Other eyewitnesses viewed the fight a little differently. They saw no
challenge from Yellow Hair. He did not know English or Lakota, and
Cody did not know Cheyenne.[36] There was no hand-to-hand combat.
However, Cody did scalp Yellow Hair and raised his scalp and headdress,
shouting, "The first scalp for Custer." The Cheyenne did not attack Cody
but retreated when they saw the advancing troops.[37] (It's interesting to
note that in the 1920 version of Cody's autobiography, all references to
his scalping the Indian were removed.)[38]

Cody continued with theatrics, eventually establishing his world-
famous Wild West show. By 1909, ticket sales had declined, so Cody
combined his Wild West with the show of his competitor Gordon Lillie,
known as Pawnee Bill.[39] In 1913, low on funds, Cody obtained a $20,000
loan from Denver entrepreneur Harry Tammen, who also wanted Cody

to perform in his Sells-Floto Circus if the note was not repaid. Pawnee Bill was furious with Cody's commitment to abandon their partnership. Tammen bought another outstanding loan of Cody and Pawnee Bill's show, and when they couldn't repay, Tammen foreclosed on the show, selling their assets.[40] Cody performed in Tammen's Sells-Floto Circus into 1915.

Cody helped found the town Cody, Wyoming, in the spring of 1896.[41] He worked to develop irrigated agriculture for the area; lived at his TE Ranch; owned the Irma Hotel, named after his daughter; and had way stations on the road to Yellowstone National Park. In his will, Cody stated that he wanted to be buried on Cedar Mountain overlooking his town.[42]

Cody died on January 10, 1917, in Denver, Colorado, while visiting his sister. Tammen wanted Cody buried on Lookout Mountain in Golden, Colorado, and requested permission from Louisa, Cody's wife. A second, more recent will by Buffalo Bill left everything to Louisa. She agreed to have Cody buried on Lookout Mountain. The people of Cody, Wyoming, were furious. A nasty rumor spread that Tammen had paid Louisa $10,000 to bury Buffalo Bill on Lookout Mountain.[43]

Buffalo Bill Cody didn't need to concoct stories, and he didn't need to embellish his accomplishments. But he did. However, he was gracious to many people and gave the world a good show.

Chapter Seven

THE DEATH OF CRAZY HORSE

JUST THE FACTS

THE *WAKINYAN*, THUNDER BEINGS, CAME TO THE BOY IN A DREAM AS HE sat alone on a hill. A horse and rider emerged out of still water. The horse changed colors as they rode untouched against an onslaught of bullets and arrows, but in the end the rider was pulled down by his own people. Such was the dream of the boy who would be named *Tasunke Witko*, or Crazy Horse. Lakota historian Joseph M. Marshall III says of Crazy Horse, "I think of him as *wica* or 'complete man.' . . . A *wica* was the kind of man who demonstrated the highest Lakota virtues of generosity, courage, fortitude, and wisdom."[1]

The boy who was first called Curly and Light Hair was born in present-day South Dakota's Black Hills, in the year a hundred horses were taken, most likely 1840.[2] He was born into the Oglala subgroup, one of the Seven Council Fires of the Lakota people. The boy grew up learning hunting and warfare.

Immigrants began traveling the Oregon Trail, and to help protect them, the federal government bought a trading post, Fort Laramie, in present-day Wyoming. In 1851, American peace commissioners held a council with plains tribes at Fort Laramie, persuading them to sign the Horse Creek treaty guaranteeing the tribes would not molest travelers along the Oregon Trail. The peace commissioners named the Brulé chief

Conquering Bear chief of all the Sioux, even though he knew he could not speak for any of the other Lakota.[3]

In 1854, Curly visited Conquering Bear's camp near Fort Laramie. A Mormon immigrant's cow wandered into camp and someone killed it. On August 19, 1854, Second Lieutenant John Grattan, along with twenty men and two howitzers, entered Conquering Bear's camp to arrest the cow killer. Conquering Bear offered to pay for the cow but refused to turn over the killer. Grattan ordered the cannons to be fired, severely wounding Conquering Bear, whose warriors quickly wiped out Grattan and his men. Curly was greatly affected by Conquering Bear's wounding and subsequent death. On September 3, 1855, Curly was visiting Little Thunder's camp on the Blue Water River in Nebraska Territory. He was away hunting when General William Harney's troops attacked, killing men, women, and children. This attack reinforced Curly's view that whites were killers and not to be trusted.

Curly later joined in a raid, killing two enemy warriors. In honor of his son's accomplishments, Curly's father gave him his own name—Crazy Horse.[4]

Crazy Horse continued his heroic exploits and was made a Shirt Wearer. Shirt Wearers lived not for themselves but for the people. He relinquished his position when he became embroiled in a personal dispute over a woman. The elders decreed that no one was ever to wear Crazy Horse's shirt again.[5] But this did not stop him from doing good deeds.

In June 1866, during peace negations at Fort Laramie, the Lakota learned that the army planned to build forts along the Bozeman Trail, running along the eastern slopes of Wyoming's Bighorn Mountains. The Lakota leader Red Cloud left the negotiations, stating that the forts and travelers would not be allowed in Lakota territory. The army built its forts anyway.

Red Cloud's Lakota concentrated their attacks against Fort Phil Kearny in Wyoming. On December 21, 1866, Crazy Horse and others acted as decoys to lure Captain William Fetterman and eighty soldiers away from the fort, where they were then cut off and killed. Red Cloud's War ended with the 1868 Fort Laramie treaty, requiring the army to abandon the Bozeman Trail forts and prohibiting whites from entering the Great Sioux Reservation, which encompassed the disputed area in Wyoming and the Black Hills.

In 1874, Lieutenant Colonel George Custer led an expedition into the Black Hills, discovering gold and triggering a gold rush. The Lakota began killing the interlopers. In the spring of 1876, three armies converged on the Lakota, who were known to be in southeastern Montana, north central Wyoming, and western Dakota Territories. General George Crook led his army from the south; General Alfred Terry, along with Custer's Seventh Cavalry, came from the east; and Colonel John Gibbon from the west.

The Lakota and Cheyenne, under Crazy Horse's leadership, attacked Crook's army on June 17, 1876. His forces fought Crook to a stalemate at the Battle of the Rosebud. On June 25, Custer attacked the massive village of Lakota, Dakota, Cheyenne, and Arapaho on the Little Bighorn River. Crazy Horse and his Oglalas, as well as many others, overwhelmed and annihilated Custer and his immediate command. Crook and Terry pursued Crazy Horse through the summer as he continued to elude them.

On January 8, 1877, General Nelson Miles's troops attacked Crazy Horse's village along the Tongue River in Montana. Crazy Horse and his warriors fought a rearguard action, bogging down the soldiers in foot-deep snow until a blizzard ended the conflict, allowing Crazy Horse's people to escape.

General Crook promised that if Crazy Horse surrendered, he could have a reservation in the Powder River Country. Crazy Horse's people were starving; he knew this was the best deal he could get, and he surrendered on May 6, 1877.

"Kill Him! Kill Him!"—Bill Markley

General George Crook was pleased. He had sent Lakota emissaries to Crazy Horse claiming that if he surrendered, he and his people would be well treated. Crazy Horse responded that they would surrender if they were given a reservation in the Powder River Country. Through further negotiations, Crazy Horse believed that he had been promised a Powder

River reservation. He agreed to surrender at Red Cloud Agency near Fort Robinson, Nebraska.

Crazy Horse arrived at Red Cloud Agency on May 6, 1877, surrendering to Crook's chief of scouts, First Lieutenant William Philo Clark. A correspondent for the *New York Tribune* reported on the event, writing:

> *The entire Crazy Horse band, consisting of about 900 Indians, surrendered here today. . . . Crazy Horse was riding a few steps in advance of the leading chiefs, while some 300 warriors . . . followed. . . . Crazy Horse and his principal men dismounted, advanced to meet Lieut. Clark, and shook hands cordially. . . . Crazy Horse told his spokesman . . . that the chieftain would make peace for all time, and that as he smoked the peace pipe he would invoke the Great Spirit to make it eternal.[6]*

Crazy Horse attempted to fit in, locating his camp near Red Cloud Agency and living peacefully. On May 12, 1877, he enlisted as an army scout, and on July 1, 1877, he was made first sergeant of Company C Indian Scouts.[7]

Crook held a council meeting near Red Cloud Agency on May 25. When it was Crazy Horse's turn to speak, he said that he had selected the site for his reservation and his people were ready to return and live there. Sadly for Crazy Horse and his people, Crook stepped back from his promise, saying, "You asked for a reservation in the upper country. . . . I cannot decide these things for myself. They must be decided in Washington." Crook said a commissioner would be taking some Lakota leaders to Washington, where they could make their case.[8]

There was talk that the Lakota would be sent south to Indian Territory (modern-day Oklahoma), but, just as bad, Crazy Horse and the other Lakota leaders learned that the government planned to move them east to the Missouri River, which had never been their territory.[9] Standing up for his people, Crazy Horse did not allow the government officials to forget that they had promised him a Powder River reservation.

The government wanted Crazy Horse to visit President Rutherford B. Hayes as part of a delegation in mid-September. He was reluctant to go; he heard that when other tribal leaders left their reservations, they were separated out and sent to Florida.

Crazy Horse requested to go on a buffalo hunt in the Powder River Country, and on July 27, Crook authorized it in a letter. But on August 5, the army canceled the buffalo hunt. They worried that if a large group of Indians left the reservations, they might make a run for it and join Sitting Bull in Canada.[10] Crazy Horse declared that since there was no buffalo hunt, he was not going to Washington. Lieutenant Clark insisted he go, but Crazy Horse was firm, declaring, "I am not going."[11]

In May, the army ordered the Nez Perce tribe to leave their eastern Oregon homelands and relocate to a reservation in Idaho Territory. The Nez Perce were reluctantly complying when a few young men murdered some settlers, sparking the Nez Perce War. The army wanted to enlist Lakota warriors to help track and capture the Nez Perce.[12]

On August 31, Clark met with Crazy Horse and Touch-the-Clouds, a Miniconjou leader from Spotted Tail Agency, roughly thirty miles east of Red Cloud Agency, requesting they fight against the Nez Perce. They said no. Both had agreed never to fight again. The interpreter Frank Grouard misinterpreted their words, saying that Touch-the-Clouds would fight alongside the Nez Perce and that Crazy Horse had said the soldiers might as well come and kill him and his people in camp because he was going north.[13]

The exchange became heated, and after an angry Grouard left, Billy Garnett, another translator, arrived and told Clark that Crazy Horse did not want to fight against the Nez Perce, but he did want to go north to hunt buffalo. Clark twice denied Crazy Horse's request.[14] Now suspicious of Crazy Horse and Touch-the-Clouds, Clark sent a message to Captain Daniel Burke, commander of Camp Sheridan near Spotted Tail Agency, writing, "Crazy Horse and Touch-the-Clouds with High Bear came up and told me that they were going north on the war-path."[15]

Clark told his concerns to Lieutenant Colonel Luther Bradley, commander of Camp Robinson. Bradley notified General Phil Sheridan, Crook's commanding officer in Chicago, who sent a telegram to Crook instructing him to personally investigate and manage the situation.[16] Crook, who was traveling to Wyoming to prepare to go after the Nez

Perce, was irritated that he had to interrupt his plans. Arriving at Camp Robinson on September 2, Crook made the decision to arrest Crazy Horse and Touch-the-Clouds.[17]

Crook was making plans for the arrests with Bradley and Clark when First Lieutenant Jesse Lee, Indian agent at Spotted Tail Agency, joined their meeting. Lee told them of Grouard's mistranslation of Crazy Horse's and Touch-the-Cloud's words. The discussion became heated between Lee and Clark, as Clark believed Grouard. Crook relented on arresting Crazy Horse for the time being, and Lee returned to Spotted Tail Agency.[18] Bradley recorded in his journal that "after consideration the movement was deferred."[19]

Crook sent word to Crazy Horse, Red Cloud, and other chiefs that he wanted to meet with them the next morning, September 3, at Red Cloud's camp to hear what Crazy Horse had to say for himself.[20] Crazy Horse responded that he would not attend because "no good would come of it."[21]

On the morning of September 3, as Crook and his escort headed toward the meeting, the interpreters Billy Garnett and Baptiste "Big Bat" Pourier intercepted them. They had the warrior Woman Dress with them, who had information for Crook. Woman Dress said that Crazy Horse planned to attend the meeting along with sixty warriors. When Crazy Horse shook Crook's hand, he would hold on, signaling his men to kill Crook and everyone with him.[22]

Crook decided to go directly to Crazy Horse's camp and confront him anyway. With Grouard again acting as translator, the meeting erupted into a heated exchange. Crook came away from the meeting believing that Crazy Horse planned to flee to Canada. Dr. Valentine McGillycuddy, a friend of Crazy Horse and assistant post surgeon at Fort Robinson, believed Grouard again had mistranslated what Crazy Horse was saying. McGillycuddy went to Crook to defend Crazy Horse and to let Crook know Grouard's translation was wrong, but Crook said no, he was sure Crazy Horse was going north to join Sitting Bull.[23]

Crook canceled the meeting at Red Cloud's camp. Later that day, Crook and Clark held a secret meeting with Red Cloud and a select few tribal leaders and they plotted to kill Crazy Horse. Bradley was not invited. Each leader was to pick four men to go after Crazy Horse that night. The man who killed Crazy Horse would receive $300 and a prized horse owned by Clark. Following the meeting, Crook resumed his trip toward Wyoming to pursue the Nez Perce.[24]

Bradley learned of the plot to kill Crazy Horse and ordered Clark to end the assassination plans. Clark was to inform the Lakota leaders that they were to report with their warriors in the morning, when they would ride with the army to Crazy Horse's camp and arrest him.[25] Crazy Horse was to be sent by rail to Omaha, then on to Florida, where he would be exiled to the Dry Tortugas, seventy miles off Florida's coast.[26]

At nine o'clock the next morning, eight companies of cavalry, supported by four hundred Indian warriors, marched on Crazy Horse's camp. Crazy Horse learned of their advance, and the village dispersed long before they got there.[27]

First Lieutenant Jesse Lee learned that Crazy Horse had arrived at Spotted Tail Agency's northern camps. Lee, Captain Daniel Burke, and interpreter Louis Bordeaux met Crazy Horse, Touch-the-Clouds, and an escort of three hundred warriors. They rode with Crazy Horse to Camp Sheridan, where Crazy Horse said he wanted to live at Spotted Tail Agency instead of Red Cloud Agency. Lee and Burke were fine with the move, but they said he would first need to go to Camp Robinson, explain the situation to Bradley, and get his permission. Lee said he would go with Crazy Horse and guarantee his protection, so Crazy Horse agreed to go.[28]

Crazy Horse appeared at Camp Sheridan the next morning, September 5, at nine o'clock. Lieutenant Lee, Touch-the-Clouds, and an escort of Indian scouts rode with Crazy Horse for Camp Robinson. Lee received a message along the way from Bradley stating that Crazy Horse needed to be taken directly to the adjutant's office. Bradley had received a message from Crook reaffirming Crazy Horse's arrest.[29]

They arrived at Camp Robinson at six o'clock that evening. Approximately eight hundred soldiers were stationed there, and now many armed Lakota warriors, some friendly to Crazy Horse and others not, clustered throughout the fort. Riding up to the adjutant's office next to the guardhouse, the group was met by Second Lieutenant Fredric Calhoun, who hated Crazy Horse. His brother James had been killed at the Little

Bighorn, along with James's brother-in-law Lieutenant Colonel George Custer.[30]

Lee said that he wanted Bradley to meet with Crazy Horse. Calhoun told Lee to turn Crazy Horse over to the officer of the day, Captain James Kennington. Lee left Crazy Horse in the adjutant's office and walked across the parade ground to Bradley's quarters. Bradley was out on his veranda and congratulated Lee on bringing in Crazy Horse. Lee asked whether Bradley could meet briefly with Crazy Horse, but he replied that he could not. Crazy Horse was to be placed in the guardhouse and then sent away. Lee asked whether Bradley would meet with Crazy Horse in the morning; Bradley said to put him in the guardhouse and that he wouldn't be hurt. Lee grasped at this as a remote possibility for a meeting.[31]

Returning to the adjutant's office, Lee told Crazy Horse that Bradley could not meet with him now, but if he went with Kennington, he would not be harmed. That seemed to satisfy Crazy Horse. A Lakota Indian policeman named Little Big Man held Crazy Horse's left hand and Captain Kennington held his right as they led him outside toward the guardhouse through the gathering crowd of Crazy Horse supporters and opponents.[32]

Entering the guardhouse, Crazy Horse saw soldiers on duty and a cell with prisoners wearing leg irons. Realizing he was going to be a prisoner, he tore loose from Little Big Man and Kennington. Little Big Man tried to restrain him as Crazy Horse pulled out his knife and slashed Little Big Man's arm. Kennington pulled out his sword, yelling to the soldiers inside the guardhouse not to shoot. Crazy Horse made it outside the door, where a guard stood with fixed bayonet.[33]

According to Lee, Kennington shouted, "Kill him! Kill him!"[34] and according to Bordeaux, Kennington shouted, "Stab the sonofabitch! Stab the sonofabitch!"[35]

The story is murky, but many say the guard stabbed Crazy Horse in his right side and he fell to the ground. Crazy Horse was carried into the adjutant's office, where his friend Dr. Valentine McGillycuddy cared for him until he died later that night.

Lieutenant Clark telegrammed Crook concerning Crazy Horse, "The death of this man will save trouble."[36] General Sheridan told reporters in Chicago, "Crazy Horse was a mischievous and dangerous malcontent,

Artist's rendition of Crazy Horse's followers on their way to surrender at Red Cloud Agency, Nebraska, Sunday, May 6, 1877. COURTESY OF DENVER PUBLIC LIBRARY, WESTERN HISTORY COLLECTION (X-33607)

and it is a good thing he is dead."[37] But Valentine McGillycuddy, Crazy Horse's friend, said:

> *Crazy Horse had the reputation among the whites and Indians generally of being a man of his word, and never breaking a promise; hence, it is my opinion that he had no intention of again going on the warpath and joining Sitting Bull, as charged at the time of his arrest. A combination of treachery, jealousy and unreliable reports simply resulted in a frame-up, and he was railroaded to his death.[38]*

THE CONSPIRACY TO ASSASSINATE CRAZY HORSE— KELLEN CUTSFORTH

Of all the Indians in the history of the American West, Crazy Horse is perhaps the greatest symbol of native resistance. He is so revered that work is under way, and has been since 1948, to create the world's largest sculpture of the Lakota warrior in the Black Hills of South Dakota near Mount Rushmore. The monument, carved out of the granite mountain-side, is estimated to be 641 feet wide and 563 feet high when finished. It is a little odd, however, that no authenticated photo of Crazy Horse exists. In fact, the sculptors of the monument have only artist renderings and historic recollections to go by for the design.

Even with these circumstances, the great Lakota warrior's sculpture will represent the man riding a horse and pointing into the distance. It is this type of mystique that adds to the legend of Crazy Horse. He was a man who marched to the beat of his own drum and was an inspiration to the Lakota people. These same attributes, however, led to the conspiracy against him and to his eventual murder.

During his life, Crazy Horse was a warrior beloved by many of the Lakota people and the men who followed him into battle. He bucked the traditions of his tribe by never counting coup, never wearing a war bonnet, and rarely attending the councils of tribal elders.[39] As a deeply spiritual man, he carried several charms and talismans to protect him from his enemies, and he never allowed any of his men to ride ahead of him into battle.[40] These attributes caused him to be very popular among Lakota warriors, but he was also known to have accumulated several enemies among his own people.

After engaging in numerous battles against enemy tribes such as the Crow and Shoshone, and against the US military as well, Crazy Horse was eventually forced to give up the warrior's path for reservation life. Both Red Cloud, a chief of the Oglala Lakota who had been living among white men for several years, and Spotted Tail, a Brulé Lakota leader and uncle to Crazy Horse, were promised their own reservations in the game-rich region of the Powder River Country in northern Wyoming if they could convince Crazy Horse to surrender.[41]

With the threat of starvation looming over his band of Indians, Crazy Horse led them to Fort Robinson, Nebraska, on May 6, 1877, to surrender.[42] He Dog, an Oglala warrior who was good friends with Crazy Horse, said of the surrender, "Spotted Tail went north and persuaded Crazy Horse to come down to the reservation the following spring. Spotted Tail had laid a trap for us. Later, I found that Spotted Tail was telling the military things about Crazy Horse which were not so."[43]

Although surrounded by questionable pretenses, Crazy Horse and his band of Lakota surrendered with the promise that he and his people would receive a reservation of their own in the north.[44] Crazy Horse and his men were then assigned a campsite between the Red Cloud and Spotted Tail Agencies.[45] Almost from the very instant he surrendered, Crazy Horse began to have second thoughts about laying down his arms. Crazy Horse also heard rumors that the Lakota were going to be removed to a new, hated Missouri River reservation.[46] Many of the young Lakota already living at the reservation, as well as Crazy Horse's men, began to identify with his attempts to resist their removal and to not completely submit to reservation life as Red Cloud and Spotted Tail had.[47]

Crazy Horse was truly a born leader and an attraction. Red Feather, the younger brother of Crazy Horse's first wife and a member of his band, said, "All the white people came to see Crazy Horse and gave him presents and money. The other Indians at the agency got very jealous."[48] Word of his leadership and popularity made Red Cloud (and perhaps Spotted Tail) not only jealous but also fearful of young Crazy Horse's political power. As historian Dale L. Walker states, "It seems clear that Red Cloud and his followers had a role in the discrediting of the famed fighter."[49]

Tensions continued to worsen between the three Lakota leaders when the men were asked to make a trip to Washington, DC, and hold a council with President Rutherford B. Hayes concerning a move to the new, dreaded Missouri River reservation.[50] Crazy Horse did not believe anything good could come from the meeting and that Red Cloud and Spotted Tail, when returning from such trips, normally returned with white men's ideas, not ideas to help their own people.[51]

Making matters worse, in August 1877, Crazy Horse and his seven-foot-tall friend Touch-the-Clouds traveled to the Red Cloud Agency to talk with Lieutenant William P. Clark about recruiting Indian scouts to help capture Chief Joseph and his band of Nez Perce Indians, who were rebelling in Idaho.[52] Assigned to translate for Crazy Horse was a hefty man named Frank Grouard, who was nicknamed "Grabber," and a second interpreter named Louis Bordeaux. During the meeting, Crazy Horse stated, in relation to helping fight the Nez Perce, that he thought the white man wanted his people to be done with war, but if the white man wanted him to fight, he would fight until there were no Nez Perce left.[53]

Grouard mistranslated Crazy Horse's final words as "until there were no *white men* left."[54] Many historians believe Grouard had been instructed by Red Cloud and Spotted Tail or some of their followers to purposely change the translation in order to cause the destruction of Crazy Horse and his leadership.[55] It is important to note that when Bordeaux heard the mistranslation, he immediately challenged Grouard's interpretation, but the damage had already been done. Clark, who was already suspicious of Crazy Horse, relayed his fears through other officers, who told General Phil Sheridan, saying, "There is a good chance for trouble here."[56]

In response to this false fear, Sheridan ordered General George Crook to go to Fort Robinson and deal with the uprising, if there was one.[57] Crook, however skeptical, made the trek to Fort Robinson to hold a special council with certain Lakota chiefs and sub-chiefs.[58] The meeting was called off, however, as an interpreter named William Garnett, who was on his way to the council, was stopped by a Lakota informant named Woman Dress, a relative and confidant of Red Cloud. This scout told Garnett that "Crazy Horse is going to come [to the meeting] with sixty Indians and catch General Crook by the hand, like he was going to shake hands, and he is going to hold on to him, and those sixty Indians are going to kill Crook and whoever is with him."[59]

Woman Dress, it is reported, received his information thirdhand. The origin of the rumor was most likely started by either the Spotted Tail or the Red Cloud contingent and was meant to destroy any remaining trust the US military officials at Fort Robinson had in Crazy Horse. His adversaries also hoped this would lead to his demise.

After this news reached Crook, his subordinates advised him to postpone the council. Shortly after canceling the council, the military learned that neither Crazy Horse nor any of his band were near the council.[60] When Crook reconvened the council, Crazy Horse did not attend; his absence infuriated Crook, who explicitly told Red Cloud and the other leaders that they needed to do something to "control" the free-spirited warrior. One of the Indian delegation said that if Crazy Horse could not be controlled, he would have to be killed.[61]

Crook responded to this idea with disdain. Although he had been an avid Indian fighter during the Sioux campaign and against several other tribes, he did not have the stomach for political killings outside of combat and advised against such action.[62] In fact, Crook's own biographer, Dan Thrapp, wrote that the general had no taste for treachery or executions. This is more proof that the plan to murder Crazy Horse had roots planted among his own people rather than in the military ranks at Fort Robinson.

The talk of killing Crazy Horse, however, continued even after Crook forbade it. The translator William Garnett, who attended the meetings, stated that each chief present at the council agreed to select four warriors from their bands to go to Crazy Horse's village and kill him. Ammunition was also passed around, and $300 and a horse were offered by one of the officers for any of the chosen Indians who did the deed.[63]

It is a fact that much of this talk and plotting came from Red Cloud's contingent. These formulated plots were quickly extinguished by officers who were thinking more clearly, and the Indians at the council were ordered not to make an attempt on Crazy Horse's life.[64] After Red Cloud's people were stopped from attempting to murder Crazy Horse, orders were issued to place Crazy Horse in prison, and he would eventually be sent to the Dry Tortugas, seventy miles off the coast of Key West.[65]

After taking council at Camp Sheridan, Crazy Horse and a large procession of people made their way to Fort Robinson, looking to negotiate with Lieutenant Colonel Bradley. Crazy Horse hoped to resume the negotiations about the original promise of a Powder River reservation. When Crazy Horse entered the fort, he was accosted by the Lakota policeman Little Big Man, who grabbed Crazy Horse by the arm and said, "Come along, you man of no-fight. You are a coward!"[66] At this point, a multitude of Lakota Indians from all of the various bands gathered around to see Crazy Horse shoved toward the adjutant's office by Little Big Man. At the head of the gathered Indian horde was Red Cloud, keeping a watchful eye on Crazy Horse.[67]

Crazy Horse soon found that he would not be able to talk with Bradley, so he was marched across the fort grounds, Little Big Man gripping his arm and a soldier walking by his other side. Two soldiers quickly walked behind them toward a building that was used as a jailhouse.[68] Many of the Indians gathered knew where they were taking the respected warrior and they began to undulate in what was described as a roar.[69] Guns were raised by the soldiers to keep the mob under control.

As Crazy Horse approached the prison, he passed a guard with a bayoneted rifle and, after looking past the guard, understood that he was not going to be waiting for a negotiation but was going to be placed in shackles and locked in a prison cell.[70] Realizing his predicament, Crazy Horse tried to resist and was grabbed by Little Big Man, who wrenched his arms behind his back. As Crazy Horse fought to free himself, he forced Little Big Man out of the doorway. Seeing this, Red Cloud shouted, "Shoot in the middle; shoot to kill!"[71]

Crazy Horse was soon able to free his arms and draw a knife he had concealed. Slashing at Little Big Man, he bloodied the policeman as two other Brulé Lakota Indians charged in to restrain him. As they did, an unidentified guard lunged with his bayoneted rifle and drove the blade deep into Crazy Horse's flesh, mortally wounding him.[72] According to Dr. Valentine McGillycuddy, who worked feverishly to save Crazy Horse's life, the great warrior died around midnight that evening.

It is clear that a conspiracy existed among Red Cloud, Spotted Tail, and many of the other reservation chiefs, who felt threatened by Crazy Horse's influence over the young men and warriors. They were jealous of the respect he received and the admiration that most of the reservation Lakota gave to him.

The sad story of the death of Crazy Horse is best summarized by Samuel Stands, an interpreter who was researching Crazy Horse's life. Around 1930, Stands interviewed a Lakota "old timer" (who would not allow his name to be divulged) who was at Fort Robinson at the time of Crazy Horse's death. This Lakota man told Stands, "I'm not telling anyone—white or Indian—what I know about the killing of Crazy Horse. That affair was a disgrace, and a dirty shame. We killed our own man."[73]

Chapter Eight

DID PAT GARRETT KILL BILLY THE KID?

JUST THE FACTS

BILLY THE KID IS ARGUABLY THE BEST-KNOWN OUTLAW IN THE HIS-
tory of the Old West. And yet his life is shrouded in myth and mystery,
and there is very little evidence of Billy's early life or even his origins.
Many diligent researchers, however, have attempted to track an individual, believed to be Billy, through sparse historical records. These
researchers believe Billy was born in 1859 in the Irish slums of Brook-
lyn, New York. He was given the name Henry by his immigrant mother,
Catherine McCarty, and had a brother named Joseph. Historians are
not clear as to whether the boys were a product of an early marriage or
just a short-lived relationship, but most believe Catherine immigrated
to America to escape Ireland's potato famine, which swept the country
in those years.

After moving around the United States, Catherine eventually married William Henry Harrison Antrim in Santa Fe, New Mexico Territory,
on March 1, 1873. Following the ceremony, the Antrim family settled in
Silver City, New Mexico Territory. Shortly thereafter, Catherine, who
had been suffering from tuberculosis, died on September 16, 1874.

Following his mother's death, young Henry's life took a turn for the
worse. He and his brother were left alone at a boardinghouse for several
months at a time, as their stepfather was busy chasing dreams of rich

mineral strikes in the surrounding territories. At a young age, Henry began using two different names: Henry Antrim and Henry McCarty. He also began to stray from a path of morality, testing the very boundaries of the law.

With the absence of parental supervision, young Henry began committing petty thievery, including stealing several pounds of butter from a rancher and a bundle of clothing from a Chinese laundry. The latter offense caused Henry to be jailed; however, he promptly escaped by shimmying up the building's chimney and out to freedom.

After his escape, Henry abandoned his family and made his way to Camp Grant in Arizona Territory. At the tender age of fifteen, Henry disappeared from the historical record for nearly two years; then he resurfaced, working as a ranch hand for the well-known cattleman Henry Hooker. With this outfit, young Henry learned to ride, rope, and punch cattle. He also learned to rustle livestock, steal saddles, and continue his petty thievery. And it was at this time that he began using the nickname "Kid."

Because of his ornery attitude, the Kid came to grief by way of a man named Francis P. Cahill. Francis, who unmercifully picked on Henry while at Camp Grant, decided to "slap the Kid around" one evening, and the young man finally had enough of the abuse. Drawing a pistol, the Kid shot Francis in the stomach, killing him.

Following this incident, Henry ran back to New Mexico Territory. Upon his return, the Kid learned to speak Spanish fluently, developed a reckless boldness and a hair-trigger temper, and became a favorite of many Mexican women. During this time, he also acquired a new alias: William H. Bonney. When combined with his old nickname of the "Kid," he quickly evolved into the famous Billy the Kid persona.

Billy eventually fell in with a young English stock raiser named John Tunstall, who had come to New Mexico to make his fortune with two business partners, Alexander McSween and famous cattleman John Chisum. Conflict soon arose between these men and their competitor James Dolan. The more established Dolan operated a dry goods monopoly in the area through a general store locally referred to as "the House." The Tunstall group opened a rival store in hopes of competing with Dolan.

Both sides eventually gathered lawmen, ranch hands, and outlaws to defend their positions. Tunstall was soon ambushed by Dolan's gang and murdered. A group calling themselves the Regulators, which included Billy, formed to avenge Tunstall. They set off what is commonly known as the Lincoln County War. This conflict devolved into back-and-forth revenge killings that eventually led to Billy's role as an accessory in the murder of Lincoln County sheriff William Brady, who had sided with Dolan's gang.

These murders caused the issue of warrants for several participants on both sides, and the Kid was charged in the deaths of three men. Following Brady's murder, all of Tunstall's supporters gathered inside Alexander McSween's house. Their opponents set fire to the home, causing the occupants to start a shoot-out. With the house completely in flames, Billy and the inhabitants fled. During the escape, McSween was shot and killed by Robert W. Beckwith, and Billy responded by killing Beckwith.

With the death of McSween, the Lincoln County War ended. Billy went on the lam and would be hunted and eventually captured by the new Lincoln County sheriff Pat Garrett. After his incarceration, Billy escaped, murdering two of Garrett's deputies in the process. He then fled to Fort Sumner, New Mexico Territory, where he would once again be tracked and hunted by the relentless lawman Garrett.

PAT GARRETT KILLS BILLY THE KID—BILL MARKLEY

Billy the Kid killed two deputies during his escape from jail in Lincoln, New Mexico. Sheriff Pat Garrett needed to track him down, but he also needed to be careful. The Kid was dangerous and had lots of supporters, especially among Hispanios.

Sheriff Garrett was in White Oaks, New Mexico, collecting taxes on April 28, 1881, when the Kid made his escape.[1] The next day, Garrett learned of the Kid's murderous breakout and returned to Lincoln on April 30.[2] That same day, he rode out of town with a few volunteers, scouting for the Kid's trail, but found nothing.

Newspapers demanded the Kid be apprehended and face justice, and New Mexico governor Lew Wallace proclaimed a $500 reward for the

Kid's capture. Garrett's plan was to wait and see where the Kid turned up. He sent out letters of inquiry and riders to see what they could learn. After receiving lots of false leads, he heard rumors that the Kid was hanging around his old haunts at Fort Sumner.

The army had built Fort Sumner in 1863 to control the Navajos and Mescalero Apaches. In 1870, the army sold the fort to Lucien Maxwell, who moved in his family and hired hands, establishing a flourishing ranching headquarters. Lucien had died in 1875, and his son Pete took over. The Kid spent lots of time at Fort Sumner, considering it a second home; so did Pat Garrett, who had lived there working as a ranch hand and bartender.

Finally, two solid pieces of information arrived. The first was a letter from reputable rancher Manuel Brazil. Garrett had sent him a letter asking about the Kid's whereabouts. Brazil replied that he believed the Kid was in the Fort Sumner area. Later, Deputy Sheriff John Poe arrived and told Garrett that he had overheard a good source also stating that the Kid was at Fort Sumner.

Garrett believed that if he went after the Kid with a large posse, the Kid would get wind of it and flee. So he decided to take only Poe and Deputy Sheriff Thomas McKinney.

Garrett and his posse left his Roswell ranch the night of July 11, heading north along the Pecos River, staying off the road and bypassing ranch houses. He did not want to chance an informant tipping off the Kid. Garrett had written Brazil, asking him to meet them the night of July 13 at the mouth of Taiban Creek. They reached the rendezvous spot that night and waited until daylight, but Brazil never showed.

They needed a new course of action to locate the Kid. Garrett and McKinney were well known. Poe had never been to Fort Sumner, so Garrett thought it would be best to send him alone to reconnoiter. If Poe did not find any information at the fort, he was to ride to Sunnyside and talk with Garrett's friend, Postmaster Milner Rudolph, who might be able to divulge the Kid's whereabouts.

When Poe rode into Fort Sumner, the residents were wary of him. He loitered about the plaza, and then he entered Beaver Smith's saloon for a bite to eat and a few drinks, but he learned nothing. Poe rode to

Sunnyside and found Rudolph, who appeared nervous, claiming he didn't know where the Kid was.[3]

That evening, Poe returned to Fort Sumner to a designated meeting site with Garrett and McKinney north of town. He reported that he had not learned anything of importance. They decided to approach the town and see if they could spot the Kid or keep watch on Paulita Maxwell's room at Pete Maxwell's house. It was rumored that the Kid was spending time with Paulita, Pete's sister. As a final move, Garrett thought he would attempt to see his old boss Pete Maxwell, who might be able to give him information on the Kid.

At about nine o'clock that night, under a bright moon, the three men walked through an orchard toward Fort Sumner's buildings. Hearing voices speaking in Spanish, they stopped. They couldn't make out what was being said, but the voices were coming from the orchard. "Soon a man arose from the ground in full view, but too far away to recognize," Garrett said. "He wore a broad-brimmed hat, a dark vest and pants, and was in his shirt sleeves." The man said something, leaped the fence, and walked into the plaza. Garrett learned later that this was Billy the Kid.[4]

They left the orchard, then circled around to Pete Maxwell's house, originally officers' quarters. Maxwell's corner bedroom was accessible from the outside. The door and windows were open to the cool night air. Inside it appeared dark. Garrett told the others to wait outside while he entered Maxwell's bedroom. Proceeding through the fence gate, Garrett stepped up onto the porch and into the house. Poe sat on the edge of the porch, while McKinney squatted on his heels outside the fence. A few moments later, a man approached Maxwell's house wearing no hat and in his stocking feet.

It was about midnight when Garrett entered Maxwell's dark bedroom. He sat down on the edge of the bed near Maxwell's pillow, woke him, and asked if he knew where the Kid was. Maxwell replied that the Kid had been around, but he didn't know whether the Kid had left. Just then they heard voices outside.

Having left the orchard earlier, the Kid returned to the home of Saval and Celsa Gutierrez (Garrett was their brother-in-law), where he was staying. The Kid asked Celsa to fix him something to eat. Maxwell had fresh beef hanging at his house, and the Kid headed there to cut off a slab for his meal. As he left the Gutierrez home, he took a knife, as well as a pistol. Walking through the gate toward the porch of Maxwell's house, the Kid saw Poe and McKinney. Startled, the Kid pulled his gun, asking, "Quién es?" (Who is it?) Not knowing that it was the Kid, Poe stood, trying to assure him that everything was fine.[5]

"Quién es?" the Kid said again. "Quién es?" He backed into the doorway of Maxwell's bedroom, disappearing; then he stuck his head out again, saying, "Quién es?" and disappeared again.[6]

Hearing the voices, Maxwell and Garrett saw a man enter the bedroom and approach the bed.

"Who is it, Pete?" Garrett asked Maxwell, but he received no answer.

"Pete, who are they?" the Kid asked Maxwell as he leaned forward, putting both hands on the bed.

"That's him!" Maxwell whispered to Garrett, who swiftly drew his single-action Colt Army revolver from its holster and pulled the hammer back. The Kid jumped back, bringing up his pistol, asking, "Quién es? Quién es?" Garrett fired his gun, lunging to the side; then he shot a second time. The man slumped to the floor, emitting a gurgling sound. Garrett ran out of the door as Maxwell tried to run too, only to get tangled in his sheets and blanket and fall to the floor. As Maxwell ran out the door, Garrett told his deputies not to shoot him. Garrett then told them he thought he had shot the Kid. Poe said that the Kid would never come there, that Garrett must have shot the wrong man. Garrett responded that it was the Kid, that he knew the Kid's voice.[7]

It was silent in the room, but no one wanted to enter and check to make sure the Kid was dead. Maxwell lit a candle, placing it in one of the bedroom's open windows. The light revealed a motionless man on the floor. Garrett and Maxwell entered the room, determined that the man was dead, and identified him as Billy the Kid.[8]

People in town had heard the gunshots, and a crowd quickly gathered outside the Maxwell house. The word spread that Pat Garrett had shot and killed Billy the Kid. The Kid had many supporters in town, and they were becoming agitated. Delvina, one of the Maxwell servants, and Jesus Silva, a Maxwell cowboy and friend of the Kid's, entered the bedroom.

When Delvina saw the Kid's face, she began to cry and curse Garrett. Paulita Maxwell came into the bedroom and stared at the Kid's face for a long time, not saying anything. The women begged Garrett to allow them to remove the Kid's body, prepare it for burial, and hold a wake. Garrett consented, and Maxwell suggested they take the body to the fort's carpenter shop.[9]

Garrett and his men kept watch during the night. They were concerned that the Kid's friends might come after them, but no one did. The next morning, Garrett had the alcalde (magistrate) Alejandro Seguro hold an inquest on the killing. Garrett needed a legal document validating that he had killed the Kid to make sure he could collect the $500 reward. Seguro selected six men for the inquest, including Saval Gutierrez and Milner Rudolph. After examining the body and Maxwell's bedroom and interviewing the only witnesses, Garrett and Maxwell, the men unanimously concluded that Pat Garrett had shot and killed William Bonney.

The men serving on the inquest board wrote, "Our judgment is that the action of said Garrett was justifiable homicide and we are united in opinion that the gratitude of all the community is due to said Garrett for his action and whom is worthy of being compensated."[10] Garrett had his legal document validating his deed, but Governor Wallace had moved on to an ambassadorship to Turkey, and the new governor, not wanting to part so fast with the cash, said he could do nothing until the legislature met. Garrett would get his money, but he would have to wait.[11]

Jesus Silva built the Kid's coffin, Vicente Otero dug the Kid's grave in the fort's old military cemetery, and most of the town turned out for the funeral.[12]

The newspapers were jubilant, but then people started asking questions. Was it honorable to shoot the Kid in a bedroom without warning? It didn't sound like a fair fight. Con artists claimed that they had the Kid's body parts. One newspaper claimed it had his trigger finger. Some doctors claimed that they each had the Kid's skull; one even claimed that he had the Kid's complete skeleton.

Garrett was determined to set the record straight. In 1882, he teamed up with Ash Upson to write a book about the Kid titled *The Authentic Life of Billy, the Kid*. Most of the book reads like a dime novel, except for those portions where Garrett had direct contact with the Kid, where it has the ring of truth. Garrett railed against those who criticized him for shooting the Kid in the dark, and he heaped scorn on those who claimed to possess the Kid's body parts. There was no mention of the possibility that Garrett had shot the wrong man. Years later, people began claiming to be the Kid. Two of the most infamous were John Miller and Oliver "Brushy Bill" Roberts, also known as William Henry Roberts.

Miller, a cowboy from Ramah, New Mexico, claimed as an old man that he was Billy the Kid, but there was no evidence to support his claim.[13]

Roberts claimed that he had spent time with Frank and Jesse James, knew the Younger brothers, and worked for Belle Starr.[14] Later in life, he toured, signing autographs with J. Frank Dalton, who claimed to be Jesse James.[15] William Morrison, Roberts's promoter, arranged a meeting on November 30, 1950, with New Mexico governor Thomas Mabry to seek a pardon. When asked several key questions, Roberts could not answer them; he had to be prompted to remember Pat Garrett's name, and he claimed that he did not kill Garrett's deputies, so most wrote him off as a fraud.[16] Roberts said it was his friend Billy Barlow whom Garrett had killed.[17] There is no record of Billy Barlow anywhere in New Mexico Territory. But Roberts's proponents persist, saying that Billy Barlow was most likely an alias. The biggest problem with the Roberts story is that if it was all a cover-up, then Garrett, Maxwell, Poe, McKinney, and most Fort Sumner residents would have to have been in on it. Knowing human nature, someone should have spilled the beans.

To sum up the short life of Billy the Kid, it's best to use Pat Garrett's own words: "Again I say that the Kid's body lies undisturbed in the grave—and I speak of what I know."[18]

BILLY . . . THE KID WHO LIVED TO A RIPE OLD AGE— KELLEN CUTSFORTH

"Quién es? Quién es?" the lips of a young man whispered through the pitch-black darkness. There was no response to his request of "Who is it?"—only silence. "Quién es?" pleaded the voice again. This time, an answer came swiftly in the form of two successive reports from a revolver, dropping the boy. As his murderer stood over him, the young man lay in a lifeless lump on the floor, enveloped by a pool of his own blood, felled by an assassin's bullet through the heart.

Supposedly, these are the last utterances and moments in the life of the Wild West's most famous outlaw, Billy the Kid. Whether going by the names Henry Antrim, Henry McCarty, William H. Bonney, or simply the Kid, this individual's legend has become one of the most notorious in the annals of the American West. In fact, Billy has become so legendary that the only authenticated photograph of him—a weathered 1880 tintype—sold at auction for $2.3 million, and a second, unauthenticated photo discovered in 2011 has been appraised at a value of nearly $5 million.[19]

When a historic figure reaches this level of fame and notoriety, myths and tales soon follow, bolstering the legend. But in some cases, the legends are real. To better investigate the claims of the buffalo-hunting bartender turned lawman, Pat Garrett, it is best to turn back the pages of history to Fort Sumner, New Mexico Territory, and the fateful July night in question.

When Garrett caught wind that the Kid was hiding out in Fort Sumner after escaping from the Lincoln County courthouse, gunning down deputies Bob Olinger and James Bell in the process, he was bound and determined to lay the Kid six feet below the cold, hard earth. While preparing to track Billy, Garrett stopped in Roswell and gathered a pair of deputies to help on the hunt: Thomas "Tip" McKinney and John W. Poe.

McKinney was a local cowboy and ranch hand, while Poe had actual experience as a lawman, having served as a deputy marshal and town sheriff in Texas.[20] Poe was familiar with the Kid's outlaw life, though he had never seen the bandit face to face, having worked for the Canadian River Cattle Association in an attempt to stop the "rampant rustling" going on in the area at the hands of Billy and his band of rustlers.[21] When the men made their way to Fort Sumner on July 14, 1881, Poe received instructions from Garrett to scout about the town for the Kid, since most people in the town knew Garrett and McKinney by sight but did not know Poe.

Billy the Kid. Photograph taken at Fort Sumner, 1880. COURTESY OF THE UNIVERSITY OF ARIZONA LIBRARY, SPECIAL COLLECTIONS

After a futile attempt to siphon information from the locals as to the Kid's whereabouts, Poe returned to where McKinney and Garrett were camped.[22] Now, seeing no other feasible options, Garrett decided to call on his friend Pete Maxwell, who was also quite friendly with Billy, to see whether he could draw out the bandit's location. After arriving at Maxwell's home around midnight, Garret entered alone, leaving his deputies on the porch.[23]

It is at this point that history becomes hazy. According to Garrett, he woke a sleeping Maxwell to inquire about the Kid when, coincidentally, a hungry Billy arrived to carve himself a slice of meat from a beef side Maxwell had hanging from his porch.[24] In Garrett's official report to the governor of New Mexico in reference to the outlaw's death, the sheriff stated, "I at once recognized the man, and knew he was the Kid, and reached behind me for my pistol."[25] Yet in Garrett's book, *The Authentic Life of Billy, the Kid*, the lawman admitted that he did not draw down on Billy until Pete Maxwell, most likely barely awake, whispered, "That's him!"[26] So which story is the right one? Did Garrett know who was in the room immediately, or did he need the groggy confirmation of a drowsy Maxwell, who could see no better than him?

Contradicting Garrett's story further, Deputy Poe wrote in his book, *The Death of Billy the Kid*, "Garrett seemed to be in doubt himself as to whom he had shot." Poe also admitted, "[I had] considerable apprehension, as I felt almost certain that someone whom we did not want had been killed."[27]

After shaking off his own suspicions, Garrett proceeded to proclaim that he had killed Billy the Kid, saying, "That was the Kid that came in here onto me, and I think I have got him."[28] Looking upon the bloody corpse crumpled on the bedroom floor, Poe gasped, "Pat, the Kid would not come to this place; you have shot the wrong man."[29] Garrett paid no mind to Poe's proclamations and went on to take credit for the Kid's death. Neither Deputy Poe nor McKinney were familiar with what Billy looked like, so they simply accepted the lawman's identification of the corpse, while Garrett responded to Poe's fears, saying, "I had made no blunder, that I knew the Kid's voice too well to be mistaken."[30] It is also important to note that McKinney later recanted his identification of the Kid's corpse and said that he believed it was not Billy whom Garrett shot that night.[31]

Most of what is known about the events of that sweltering summer night come from two sources: Garrett's *Authentic Life* and Poe's *The Death of Billy the Kid*.[32] Garrett's book was ghostwritten by Marshal Ashmun "Ash" Upson, an itinerant journalist and former postmaster. For decades after its publication, the volume was treated as the absolute first and final authority on the life of the Kid. But following its tenth reprinting in 1976, many began to scrutinize the tales told within its pages.[33] Historians have since considered the book full of embellishments and flat-out lies concerning the life of Billy the Kid, especially when it's compared to primary resources and separate authentic accounts.

Further complicating Garrett's account of events is Poe's supposed corroborating text. In his *The Death of Billy the Kid*, there are multiple contradictions between his and Garrett's accounts of that fateful night. Some of the more glaring examples include Garrett's testimony that he saw a figure in the orchard near Pete Maxwell's estate that he later claimed was the Kid, only to turn right around, contradicting himself and writing "the Kid, by me unrecognized" about the mysterious individual in the orchard. And in the case of Poe's version, he does not mention the shadowy figure in the orchard at all.[34]

There is contradictory information as to how Billy entered the room, how his supposed corpse lay on the floor, and whether he had a pistol on his person. The stories also diverge when it comes to how the lawmen happened upon the whereabouts of the Kid. Garrett states that he received a letter from a person divulging Billy's hiding place, whereas Poe says that he himself informed Garrett of the Kid's hideout after learning the location from a Texas man.[35] Some reliable accounts of the event state that the body of the man killed in Pete Maxwell's bedroom lay there until the following morning, when a court of inquiry could inspect the corpse. However, in Poe's account he states that women came and took the body to a place where it could be surrounded by candles in a "wake" ceremony.[36] This is just another contradiction in a list of inaccuracies.

Why is there so much misinformation from two individuals who were both on the scene of this now-historic event? Is there a possibility that the man shot that night was not the Kid? But if the man killed that hot summer evening was not Billy the Kid, then who was it, and what became of the wild young outlaw?

In 1948, William V. Morrison, a paralegal case worker and avid researcher of New Mexico history, was working in a small Texas town when he was approached by a man who said Billy the Kid was still alive and living in the town of Hamilton, Texas.[37]

Following up on the lead, Morrison confronted an elderly man going by the name William Henry "Brushy Bill" Roberts, asking him whether he was in fact Billy the Kid. At first, the old man denied he was the outlaw, but after much cajoling by Morrison, Brushy Bill admitted that he was the notorious bandit.[38] Amazed at what he had just unearthed, Morrison began conducting a series of interviews with Roberts in which they discussed the events of Billy the Kid's life.

Besides matching the physical description of the Kid, Roberts also knew some very intimate details about Billy's life. The old man described people, places, and events in detail and accurately. He also had intimate knowledge of the Lincoln County War and the involvement of Alexander McSween and dry goods monopoly operator Lawrence Murphy. In one of the interviews, Roberts told Morrison, "Lawyer McSween had been hired by the Murphy bunch to prosecute some of the [John] Chisum cows that were stolen by Murphy's men." He went on to state, "McSween switched sides and 'joined up with [John] Tunstall.'"[39]

Roberts's knowledge extended not only to the factional split between the dry goods businessmen but also to the death of John Tunstall, the formation of the Regulators, and the eventual Lincoln County War. What made all this remarkable was that Roberts was nearly illiterate and would not have been able to read any of the literature produced on the subject up to that point. Yet his memory and the details he relayed to Morrison were surprisingly accurate. Brushy Bill also said that the man killed that summer night in 1881 was a man going under the alias Billy Barlow who was a friend of the Kid's and part of his rustler gang.[40]

Morrison, enamored by the stories told by Brushy Bill, helped set up a hearing for Roberts in New Mexico to receive a pardon for the murder of Sheriff William Brady. A pardon had originally been promised to the Kid by New Mexican territorial governor Lew Wallace. When the court date came, Morrison and Roberts received much notoriety as well as criticism. After the hoopla leading up to their day in court, a forty-five-minute interview was conducted wherein the now ninety-one-year-old Roberts had difficulty answering questions without prompting. After the interview, the court denied Roberts a pardon and questioned whether he had any claim to it, as the judge believed that he was not Billy the Kid.[41]

Further questions about Roberts's legitimacy came over his lack of buckteeth, prominent in Billy's photo; the fact that he could not speak

Spanish; and the fact that the man Roberts claimed had been killed, Billy Barlow, was not on any Lincoln County census records.

Morrison's background also complicated matters. He was not an expert researcher or interviewer, so during his dialogue with Roberts, he neglected to follow guidelines that many historians abide by when conducting an oral history. However, he did accurately record the information told to him. This, nevertheless, is used to discredit Morrison's and Roberts's claims.

In response to the accusations, many Brushy Bill researchers point to the fact that most of Roberts's teeth had been removed when photos of him were taken. They also note that there are no verified documents containing Billy's actual handwriting, as he was believed to be barely literate, much like Brushy Bill. Also, Roberts researchers say the supposed man killed by Garrett, Billy Barlow, was an alias, much like the multiple aliases proven to be used by the Kid. And multiple sources confirm that Roberts could indeed speak Spanish.[42]

As to Roberts's inability to answer Governor Mabry's questions without coaxing, the man was ninety-one years old and facing a firing squad of questions. Perhaps he should be given the benefit of the doubt as an elderly man talking about a subject he had not broached with more than a few people in six decades.

Alongside the accusations, there have also been numerous attempts to employ forensic technology to determine Roberts's real identity. In 1990, the University of Texas used a photo-comparison computer program to overlay the one authenticated photo of Billy and a photo of Roberts. The techniques used were ones used by criminologists when identifying suspects. An expert analyst who reviewed the photos gave this assessment: "The similarity between facial structures of . . . Roberts and the man in the . . . tintype is indeed amazing."[43]

There have also been numerous attempts at DNA testing involving Billy's supposed mother, Catherine, as well as attempts to posthumously pardon the Kid and create an official death certificate, which was never produced in 1881 (for some odd reason). Most of these attempts have produced inconclusive results. One thing that is conclusive, however, is that we may never know how the Kid met his end.

Chapter Nine

GERONIMO!

JUST THE FACTS

THE NAME *GOYAHKLA* IN ENGLISH MEANS "ONE WHO YAWNS." GOYAHKLA was originally born into the Bedonkohe band of the Apache. Through marriage, he later became a warrior leader of the Chiricahua band of Apaches in what is today the state of Arizona. However, he is probably best known by the Spanish-language name the Mexican people gave him: Geronimo. In English, the name is pronounced "Jerome" and is derived from a Greek word meaning "sacred name." The Spanish pronunciation "Geronimo," however, became so associated with this warrior that it is perhaps one of the most well-known names of any Indian in American history. The origin of the name was said to come from Mexican soldiers screaming for Saint "Jerome" while being surrounded by Apaches. Another legend says the name came from a mispronunciation of Goyahkla's real name.[1] Either way, the name Geronimo stuck and eventually became famous. And in the late nineteenth century, the very mention of this name evoked terror in the hearts of Americans, Mexicans, and even other Apaches.

Born in 1829, Geronimo was a precocious boy. As he moved into young adulthood at the age of seventeen, he married and started a family.[2] But not long after this time, Geronimo's mother, first wife, and three of his children were killed by Mexicans in a raid on his Apache camp.[3]

After their deaths, Geronimo married into the Chiricahua band of the Apaches while continuing to harbor an intense hatred of Mexicans.[4]

The most pivotal moments in the lives of Geronimo and all Apaches came when the Mexican-American War ended in 1848, with the signing of the Treaty of Guadalupe Hidalgo, and with the Gadsden Purchase in 1853. These two pieces of legislation allowed the United States to acquire much of the Apaches' homeland in what would become modern-day Arizona.

Before these events, the Apaches had lived in the southwest United States and northern Mexico for hundreds of years in what is referred to as Apacheara. This was a mountainous region where the Apache moved and hunted freely. As a member of the Chiricahua band, Geronimo served under the well-known chief Cochise. When the great leader died in 1874, Geronimo took over virtual leadership of the band.[5] Although he assumed control, he had very little ambition to become chief and deferred to Naiche, the hereditary chief who was the son of Cochise.[6]

From 1858 to 1886, Geronimo waged war against Mexicans and Americans alike.[7] Part of being an Apache was raiding and war. Apaches often raided rival tribes for food and supplies and killed many through intertribal warfare. In the Apache culture, war meant full-out destruction and usually initiated revenge killings.

The Spanish and later the Mexicans had a volatile relationship with the Apaches. The Mexican state of Chihuahua tried to appease and establish a fragile peace with them; conversely, the Mexican state of Sonora engaged in constant warfare against the Apaches. In war, Geronimo was an indiscriminate killer, using a lever-action rifle, a Colt single-shot pistol, and a bowie knife.[8]

When Arizona Territory became part of the United States, initially there were peaceful relations between both sides. But as American miners entered deeper into Apacheara, mistreatment and killings on both sides became prevalent. In 1876, the US government forced the Apaches from their homeland and onto the San Carlos reservation in the southeastern portion of the territory.[9] Due to the deplorable health and environmental conditions on the reservation, it quickly became known as "Hell's Forty Acres."

General George Crook meeting with Geronimo and other Apache leaders in Canyon de los Embudos, Mexico, on March 25, 1886. C. S. Fly took this photo showing Geronimo sitting third from the left and General Crook second from the right.
COURTESY OF DENVER PUBLIC LIBRARY, WESTERN HISTORY COLLECTION (X-32942)

Geronimo lashed out against this hell and "jumped" the reservation in 1881 with seven hundred Apache warriors, traveling deep into Mexico as an act of rebellion. He was eventually joined by another seven hundred Apaches, creating a formidable force.[10] They raided and attacked settlements on both sides of the border. To deal with the problem, the American government employed General George Crook and a large military force with two hundred Apache scouts to aid in the capture of Geronimo.[11]

For two years, Geronimo and his warriors evaded capture before voluntarily returning to the San Carlos reservation in 1883. Then, in 1885, Naiche and Geronimo abandoned the reservation once again, making their way to Mexico, but with a much smaller force of warriors. Geronimo was chased by Crook yet again, and he evaded capture yet again.

Geronimo. Photograph taken by Frank Randall of the *New York Herald* in 1884 at the San Carlos reservation, Arizona. COURTESY OF DENVER PUBLIC LIBRARY, WESTERN HISTORY COLLECTION (X-32883)

Eventually, Crook was relieved of command, and Brigadier General Nelson Miles took charge. Miles soon negotiated Geronimo's surrender.[12] The army declared Geronimo a prisoner of war, and he was confined to Fort Pickens, Florida; then transferred to Mount Vernon Barracks, Alabama; and finally settled at Fort Sill, Oklahoma Territory. During this period, Geronimo became a celebrity and traveled all over the country until his death in 1909.

GERONIMO . . . THE TERRORIST——KELLEN CUTSFORTH

David Roberts once wrote about Geronimo, "No more interesting or contradictory figure crossed the stage of Western history in the second half of the nineteenth century."[13] He was right. The name Geronimo seems to resonate with the public today. Even those who know very little about him or the history of the American West seem to revere the man as a heroic figure fighting for all that is just and good in the world—a sort of David facing the unstoppable Goliath. His purported mystical qualities included visions of invulnerability to bullets. These visions gave Geronimo an almost magical and godlike status.

Geronimo, like many men, was a complex individual. He was not a black-and-white being standing on the side of good or bad. The events of his life, as a young man and into old age, made him the person he became. But instead of delving into the man's entire life and regurgitating biographical information, which has been done many times before, let us cut to the chase and review his battle tactics.

In 1850, after his children and first wife were killed, Geronimo led a band of two hundred Apaches near the town of Arizpe in the Mexican state of Sonora.[14] Geronimo insisted that the settlement they approached held the Mexicans who had massacred his family. A pitched battle ensued that involved one hundred Mexican infantry and cavalry troops. In the end, the Apaches surrounded and killed many of them, with Geronimo himself murdering several Mexicans. This act alone should have quenched his thirst for vengeance, but it did not. Geronimo harbored hatred in his heart for the Mexican people until the day he died.[15]

After the battle near Arizpe, Geronimo raided into Mexico for ten straight years. He was almost always the instigator of these raids.[16] The raids brought down many depredations on the heads of Mexican people who had nothing to do with the death of Geronimo's family members or the destruction of his tribe. Geronimo killed and pillaged indiscriminately solely because the people were Mexican.

It is also interesting to note that Geronimo remarried within nine months of the Arizpe battle and would ultimately have a total of nine wives, with as many as three at once.[17] So it seems that he was able to move on to other women but not to forgive an entire people for his first wife's death.

In a description of one of the many raids he perpetrated, with thirty warriors following him, Geronimo said, "[We captured] all the horses, mules, and cattle we wanted. . . . During this raid we killed about fifty Mexicans."[18] Again, this raid was waged not against a military installation but against civilians who had little to do with any of the Apaches. Much of what is known about Geronimo's raids into Mexico from 1851 to 1861 comes from his memoirs.[19] But even in his own reminiscences he is honest about the civilians he enjoyed killing.

By the early 1860s, the Apaches not only had been raiding the Mexicans on numerous occasions but also began to encounter white people, who were appearing in Apacheara. Many of these white men were miners looking for precious metals in the rocky and mountainous areas of Arizona Territory.

On February 5, 1861, what was known as the Bascom Affair took place in Arizona Territory. The incident was precipitated by a raid in which Apaches fell upon a small ranch on the US side of the border, stealing several head of livestock and kidnapping a twelve-year-old boy.[20] Up until this incident, the Apaches had had very little contact with Americans. The aggrieved rancher reported the kidnapping and theft to the local military establishment. With that information in hand, Lieutenant George Nicholas Bascom, with several infantry troops, rode out to bring the young boy back.

After an unsuccessful search, Bascom convinced Chief Cochise to meet with him and discuss returning the boy. Cochise arrived with his wife, brother, two nephews, and children. When negotiations deteriorated because the boy was taken by Coyotero Apaches and not Cochise's Chiricahua band, Bascom attempted to arrest Cochise. But the Apache leader escaped by slicing through the tent they were negotiating in. The rest of his relatives, however, were captured.[21]

When Cochise begged for his family's release, Bascom replied, "[Your family] would be set free just so soon as the boy was released."[22] In response, Cochise and several Apache warriors attacked a group of unaware American and Mexican teamsters. The Apaches tortured and slaughtered the Mexicans; then Cochise offered Bascom the Americans in exchange for his family members. Bascom said he would accept nothing less than the release of the boy.

Enraged, Cochise fled with his captives into Sonora and tortured, mutilated, and murdered the Americans on his way there. After finding out about the massacre, the American military hanged Cochise's brother and nephews. This angered Cochise even more and led to what is historically known as the Apache Wars. The young boy who was kidnapped, starting the war, was later found living with the Coyotero Apaches, and he would grow up to become a scout for the US military known as Mickey Free.[23] Geronimo, for his part in the affair, is said to have been one of the murderous torturers of the Mexican and American teamsters.

The *Merriam-Webster Dictionary* defines the term *terrorism* as "the unlawful use or threat of violence especially against the state or the public as a politically motivated means of attack or coercion."[24] Throughout the Apache Wars, Geronimo personified this definition. In 1882, Geronimo committed one of his worst depredations—the attack on Ash Flat.

Ash Flat was a ranch near Safford, Arizona, which was owned by a white man who was married to an Apache woman. When Geronimo and his band raided the ranch hands' lodgings, he discovered a White Mountain Apache named Bylas, who was related to the rancher's wife. Bylas worked alongside and was friendly with the white and Mexican ranchmen. Also among the ranchmen was a Mexican foreman named Mestas, his wife, and their three children, as well as two other Mexican women.[25]

Initially, Geronimo pretended to be their friend and told them that he would only take some livestock. His band, however, began killing sheep, and Geronimo slaughtered one of the rancher's son's favorite ponies. Then, with no provocation, he ordered his warriors to bind the hands and feet of the ranch hands, Mestas, his wife, two of Mestas's sons, and the Mexican women.[26]

Bylas, fearing for Mestas and his family, pleaded with Geronimo to spare their lives. He said, "Geronimo, you promised Mestas you would not injure any of them, and now you are going to kill them. If you are going to kill the Mexicans let Mestas and his family go."[27] Geronimo would hear none of it. Mestas's family were eventually tied together with a long rope and led to a hill, where they were shot and stabbed to death one by one, along with the two women and Mexican ranchmen.

Mestas's third son initially hid himself from the murderous Geronimo but was found and was going to be murdered until Naiche stepped in, stopping the slaughter. According to some newspaper accounts, Mestas was mercilessly tortured by Geronimo and his band, and when they grew tired of tormenting the Mexican, one of the Apaches buried an axe in his head.[28] Although this account's validity can be questioned, it is a fact that Mestas, most of his family, and the ranchmen were massacred for no reason. They were civilians murdered as proof of Geronimo's bloodlust. Many accounts verify these killings at the hands of the Apache war leader.

Several other newspaper accounts also told of depredations committed upon civilians by Geronimo. Some reports exaggerated Geronimo's 1882 violence, but it is quite clear that he participated in numerous atrocities, all of which were perpetrated on civilians. Apparently, during this time Geronimo attacked another ranch, killed three adults, and took a sixteen-year-old girl captive; then he grabbed a small child "by the legs and battered its brains out against the house."[29]

Though the Apaches were nomadic raiders who made a keen distinction between war for supplies and war for vengeance, Geronimo seemed to take his lust for vengeance to a new level. Many of his own people found his tactics deplorable. He was once described by First Lieutenant Britton Davis as "a thoroughly vicious, intractable, and treacherous man. [His] word, no matter how earnestly pledged, was worthless. . . . His only redeeming traits were courage and determination."[30] And army lieutenant Thomas Cruse went so far as to swear "even the Apaches thoroughly disliked and distrusted Geronimo."[31]

It is also interesting to note that many of the depredations Geronimo committed were not against the white American men and women coming into Apacheara but against Mexicans. In fact, when posed with the question, near the end of his life, as to whether he had any regrets, Geronimo responded, "I'm sorry I did not kill more Mexicans."[32]

If one is to review the life of Geronimo, one must be brutally honest when studying the facts. For much of his lifetime, Geronimo was considered the greatest terrorist in America. But these days, through much revisionist history, he has morphed into an undaunted "guerrilla" warrior whose famously brave troops were the last American Indian force to hold out against the United States.[33]

Geronimo is normally forgiven for his brutal tactics against civilians because of the equally brutal deaths of his family members at the hands of the Mexican military when he was a young man. What was done to his family by Mexican troops was inexcusable, but it did not give him carte blanche to slaughter innocent civilians who had absolutely nothing to do with the atrocities committed against him. Slaughtering infants, ruthlessly torturing captives to death, and murdering entire families like the Mestases to instill fear and control is an act of terror, plain and simple.

It is debatable whether Geronimo had the Apache people's best interests in mind when he conducted numerous violent raids. He very well may have. What is not debatable, however, are the tactics he used to represent those interests. Instead of attacking military installations, he consistently and brutally attacked and stole from civilians, which many are correct to interpret as terrorist actions.

GERONIMO'S FIGHT FOR FREEDOM—BILL MARKLEY

Geronimo's favorite sister, Ishton, was in desperate straits during childbirth. Many believed that she would die. Alone, Geronimo climbed a mountain to pray to Usen, the Supreme Being. He fasted, praying four days and nights for the lives of Ishton and the baby. On the fifth day, an unseen spiritual power spoke to him, saying they would live. The power then told him that no weapon would kill him and he would live to an old age. Ishton recovered and gave birth to a healthy baby boy, and Geronimo lived to an old age.[34]

Geronimo was the complete Apache, trained in all ways Apache from boyhood. He was a member of the warlike Chiricahua Apaches. They lived along the Gila River and in the Mogollon Mountains of eastern Arizona and western New Mexico but ranged wherever they wanted, descending into Mexico to raid and trade.

Geronimo trained as other Apache boys did for endurance, raiding, and war. He ran through the desert and over rough terrain, not eating, not drinking, and holding water in his mouth, disciplined not to swallow. To be a warrior, he had to participate in four raids, which he did. He learned of the Apache gods and Chiricahua tales, dances, and rituals. He was taught to pray to the Supreme God, Usen, who gave gifts of strength, health, and wisdom.[35]

He was not a chief. Chiefs were hereditary. But he was a powerful leader, and people listened to him because of his power. People believed he had power to heal, power to predict the future, and power to know what was happening at great distances.

Geronimo's father died when he was a young boy. His mother never remarried, and he cared for her for the rest of her life.[36]

At age seventeen, Geronimo was admitted to the warriors' council, which meant he could join other men on the warpath. "I hoped soon to serve my people in battle," he said. Geronimo and the beautiful Alope had been in love for a long time, and now he could marry her, but first her father required many ponies for her hand in marriage. Geronimo disappeared from the village, returning days later with a large pony herd that he gave to Alope's father. They made a home together and had three children. "We followed the traditions of our fathers," Geronimo said, "and were happy."[37]

The Spanish and later the Mexicans fought with Apaches for years. Mexicans were known to make overtures of peace and trade, inviting Apaches to feast and offering strong drink. Once the Apaches were drunk, however, the Mexicans would attack, killing as many men as possible and carrying off women and children to sell into slavery. The

Apaches were just as bad, attacking farms and villages. The Mexican states of Sonora and Chihuahua suffered the most from Apache raids. Even so, from time to time, Mexicans and Apaches made peace to trade.

The great Chiricahua chief Mangas Coloradas led his band, including Geronimo's family, into Chihuahua, camping outside the town of Janos. The people of Janos wanted peace and to trade with the Apaches. For several days, the townspeople provided them with food and strong drink.

The Sonoran military commander José María Carrasco led four hundred troops into Chihuahua, searching for Apache raiders. They found Mangas Coloradas's camp outside Janos. On March 5, 1851, while most of the men, including Geronimo, were in town trading, eating, and drinking, Carrasco's troops attacked the camp, killing the guards and many women and children while capturing fifty-six of them to be sold into slavery. When Geronimo returned to camp, he found Alope, their three children, and his mother dead. From that time onward, he bore an unrelenting hatred for Mexicans.[38]

He led revenge attacks against Sonoran military and towns. For the rest of his life, most of his raids and attacks were against Mexicans, although in later years he did attack Americans in New Mexico and Arizona.

Apache relations with Americans started on cordial terms but deteriorated over time until they exploded into war after the army attempted to take Cochise hostage and hanged his brother, two nephews, and three others. The humiliating whipping of Mangas Coloradas, and later his deceptive capture and murder by the army, was exacerbated even further by his beheading, followed by the boiling of the head to remove flesh and brain from the skull. These insults drove Apaches to full-scale war, with Geronimo in the thick of the fighting.

Through the efforts of people such as Tom Jeffords, Apaches began to return to a wary coexistence with Americans. In 1872, President Ulysses Grant sent General Oliver O. Howard, nicknamed the Christian General, to make peace with the Apaches, which he did with Cochise and his Chiricahuas. Howard had the president's authority to give the Chiricahuas a reservation in their traditional homeland. Cochise asked that Jeffords be their agent, and Howard agreed to that request.[39] Geronimo said of Howard, "He always kept his word with us and treated us as brothers. . . . We could have lived forever at peace with him."[40]

Apache raiding continued in Mexico. Many claimed that the Chiricahuas were the raiders, using their American reservation as a base of operations. In March 1876, Chiricahua raiders did return from Mexico. Using gold and silver, they bought whiskey from Nick Rogers, a trader on the reservation. In a drunken stupor, one of them killed two of his own sisters. Returning to Rogers's post, they demanded more whiskey. When Rogers replied that he had none, they shot and killed him and his cook.

Many Arizonans and army officers disliked Jeffords, and, using this incident, they called for his removal as the Chiricahua agent in June 1876. The commissioner of Indian Affairs instructed John Clum, agent for the San Carlos Apache Reservation (who would later become a leading figure in Tombstone, Arizona), to relieve Jeffords of his duties. The commissioner also told Clum to shut down the Chiricahua reservation and move them to the San Carlos reservation with other Apaches. Clum claimed that Geronimo had agreed to go to San Carlos, but Geronimo and many other Chiricahua leaders did not want to, and, with seven hundred warriors and their families, they fled across the border into Mexico. Clum was angry that Geronimo had duped him and became obsessed with capturing and punishing him.[41]

During the winter of 1877, Geronimo returned across the border to the Warm Springs Agency in New Mexico, driving a herd of livestock. Learning of Geronimo's return, Clum traveled to Warm Springs with more than one hundred Apache police. Through Apache messengers, Clum invited Geronimo to come in for a talk. Geronimo believed it would be a peaceful talk, as the messengers seemed friendly. When Geronimo and his men arrived, Clum surrounded them with Apache police and arrested him. Clum shackled Geronimo and six of his men in leg irons and transported them by wagon to San Carlos. More than 450 of Geronimo's people followed him to the reservation. Geronimo and his six men were kept shackled in the guardhouse for two months.[42] No charges were brought against Geronimo, and he never stood trial.

Geronimo lived for a time at San Carlos, but he and the other Chiricahuas did not like the climate or the area. It was not home. Adding to their disgruntlement, they were given shoddy supplies and shortchanged on food allotments through mismanagement and contractor greed. On April 4, 1878, Geronimo participated in a drinking spree during which he criticized a nephew, who killed himself. Remorseful, Geronimo left for Mexico but returned to San Carlos in 1880.

In 1881, an Apache holy man, Nock-ay-det-klinne, the Dreamer, prophesied that dead Apache leaders would return and the white men would vanish. The government believed that the Dreamer was dangerous and sent troops to arrest him. A fight broke out, and the Dreamer was killed. A month after the Dreamer's death, Geronimo and more than seventy men, women, and children fled to Mexico. The army was increasing troop numbers in response to the Dreamer's death, and Geronimo believed rumors that he was to be arrested.[43]

On September 4, 1882, General George Crook returned to command the Department of Arizona after serving in the northern plains' Sioux Wars. The United States and Mexico had made a treaty allowing each other's troops to cross into the other country if pursuing marauding Indians. In May 1883, Crook had his excuse to cross into Mexico. His army captured Geronimo's women and children, forcing him to talk. Geronimo and Crook held several parlays and agreed that Geronimo and his people would return to San Carlos. Geronimo said he needed to stay behind to collect the rest of his people in the mountains, and then he would bring them to the reservation. When Geronimo did return after eight months, he brought along a herd of Mexican horses and cattle that he had gathered. Crook sold Geronimo's livestock and gave the proceeds to the Mexican government to distribute to the livestock's owners.[44] Geronimo never forgave Crook for that action.

The Apaches brewed an alcoholic beverage made from corn called *tiswin*. On May 17, 1885, Geronimo and others fled San Carlos for Mexico after a *tiswin* drinking spree. According to Geronimo,

Sometime before I left, an Indian named Wadiskay had a talk with me. He said, "They are going to arrest you," but I paid no attention to

him, knowing I had done no wrong; and the wife of Mangas [son of Mangas Coloradas], Huera, told me that they were going to seize me and put me and Mangas in the guardhouse, and I learned from the American and Apache soldiers, from Chato, and Mickey Free, that the Americans were going to arrest me and hang me, and so I left.[45]

Crook again chased the Chiricahuas into Mexico. On March 25, 1886, Geronimo and the Apache chiefs met with Crook, who told them they must surrender without condition and be sent as prisoners to Florida. The Apaches bargained with Crook, asking that they be allowed to return to their reservation after two years. Crook agreed, believing he could convince Washington, but, alas, it was not to be. Washington refused their return after two years. The Apaches did not know this when they returned to the United States. Near Fort Bowie, a trader plied Geronimo and others with whiskey, telling them that the citizens of Arizona planned to hang them. Geronimo and Naiche (Cochise's son), along with thirty men, women, and children, fled back to Mexico.[46]

Headquarters reprimanded Crook for losing Geronimo. He requested reassignment, which was granted immediately. General Nelson A. Miles replaced Crook. Miles's troops relentlessly pursued Geronimo into Mexico during the summer of 1886. Plans were in place to move all Chiricahuas to Florida, even those who served the army as scouts.

Apache scouts and Miles's troops found Geronimo and convinced him to return with them to meet with Miles. Miles told Geronimo that all Chiricahuas, including his family members, had been sent to Florida. Miles told him, "Lay down your arms and come with me to Fort Bowie and in five days you will see your families now in Florida."[47] Geronimo agreed and surrendered.

Earlier, 434 Chiricahua men women and children had been sent to Fort Monroe, Florida, crowded into railroad cars, with windows locked and no access to toilet facilities.[48] Geronimo and his men were sent to Fort Pickens, Florida. Months later, they were reunited with the rest of the Chiricahuas who had been moved to Mount Vernon Barracks, Alabama. Living conditions in Florida and Alabama were not conducive to the Chiricahuas' health, and many died. They were finally sent to Fort Sill, Oklahoma, in October 1894.

Geronimo dedicated his memoirs to President Theodore Roosevelt, writing, "If I must die in bondage—I hope that the remnant of the Apache tribe may, when I am gone, be granted the one privilege which they request—to return to Arizona."[49]

Geronimo remained a prisoner of war to his dying day in 1909. After his death, his people were given the choice of staying at Fort Sill or returning to their native land in Arizona—many returned, but Geronimo's bones remain at Fort Sill.

Chapter Ten

JOHNSON COUNTY WAR— CATTLE BARONS VERSUS RUSTLERS

JUST THE FACTS

MEN WILL KILL EACH OTHER OVER ANYTHING. IN THE CASE OF WYOming's Johnson County War, men killed to control grazing land and cattle. Land disputes are as old as the American frontier, and cattle and horse theft are as old as the first American colonies. The Johnson County War was one of many chapters in this age-old story.

In 1867, the Union Pacific, in its race with the Central Pacific to build the first transcontinental railroad, had reached southeastern Wyoming Territory. Grenville Dodge, chief engineer for the Union Pacific, laid out a town site, naming it for one of the plains tribes, Cheyenne. The town grew into a major railroad hub.[1] Local cattle could now be shipped to eastern markets, and Wyoming's cattle industry boomed.

The Wyoming Stock Growers Association, the second oldest cattlemen's association in the United States, was organized on April 4, 1872, to advance and protect the interests of livestock producers.[2] The association became a powerful political organization, attracting wealthy cattle barons from as far away as Boston and New York, and even across the Atlantic to Great Britain. Wyoming achieved statehood on July 10, 1890, with Cheyenne becoming the capital. The association controlled the state government, with many of its members serving as legislators and government officials.

Livestock was big business for the cattle barons. Some did live at their ranches; others hired ranch managers to run things. When in Cheyenne, they gathered at the posh Cheyenne Club, where they could dine on the latest cuisine, play billiards, or chat while smoking cigars and sipping liquors.[3]

The lush grasslands of the open range watered by clear flowing streams along the eastern foothills of Wyoming's Bighorn Mountains were well suited for beef cattle. Much of this area lay within what would become Johnson County. The federal government built Fort McKinney in 1878 to help control Indian tribes. With the demise of the large buffalo herds and settlement of Indians on reservations, cattlemen brought their herds to Johnson County. The small town of Buffalo, established near Fort McKinney, soon grew into Johnson County's most important commercial hub and became the county seat in 1881. Large ranching operations, as well as small homesteading ranchers, ran cattle on Johnson County's grasslands.

Cattle roamed the open range unrestricted, making it necessary for cattlemen to brand their animals to show ownership. During roundups, ranch hands would determine which calves belonged to which mother cows and brand calves accordingly. Any unmarked animals were called *mavericks*, and these would also be branded. Rustling was always a concern for everyone. Cattlemen hired stock detectives to apprehend and bring rustlers to justice, but historians have found little evidence of livestock theft in the early days of Johnson County.[4]

In 1884, the Wyoming Legislature passed the Maverick Act, which gave the association all mavericks and unbranded calves and the right to determine who owned the animals. "Ranchers who asserted their right to gather mavericks from their own herds and mother cows were now rustlers," says Earl Madsen, present-day owner of Wyoming's TA Ranch.[5]

The cattle barons blamed rustlers for losses to their herds. They believed homesteading ranchers and even their own cowboys who owned personal livestock were guilty of rustling cattle from them.

Cattle barons began to forbid their employees to own livestock. They excluded homesteading ranchers from the association and from its roundups. Many Johnson County citizens saw the association's actions as attempts to drive homesteading ranchers from the open range granted to them under the federal Homestead Act and the federal Desert Land Act.

WHO CARES ABOUT THE RULE OF LAW?——BILL MARKLEY

In 1889, Johnson County juries failed to convict persons accused of rustling in five separate cases, infuriating the cattle barons. Jury members saw the evidence against the alleged rustlers as flimsy at best.

That same year, cattlemen lynched Carbon County homesteaders Ellen Watson and Jim Averell. Watson and Averell had been homesteading 480 acres of spring-fed grassland that prominent rancher Albert Bothell had previously used and wanted back. On July 20, Bothell and five other big cattlemen tore down Watson and Averell's barbed wire fence, carted off Watson and Averell, and hanged them together from a tree. Witnesses identified the murderers, but newspapers controlled by Wyoming Stock Growers Association members went to work, nicknaming Ellen Watson "Cattle Kate." Claims were made that Averell and Watson were rustlers and that Watson, the only woman ever hanged in Wyoming Territory, traded sexual favors for cattle. The accused ranchers were never indicted.[6]

Adding to the violence, in 1891 the association targeted Thomas Waggoner, a gruff German immigrant who lived in eastern Wyoming's Weston County. Waggoner, a sharp horse trader, had accumulated more than a thousand horses. On June 4, 1891, three men rode up to Waggoner's cabin and arrested him for horse theft. They told his wife that they were taking him to jail in Newcastle, Wyoming. For days, Waggoner's wife had no word from him. When she learned that he had never arrived in Newcastle, a search team scoured the countryside. On June 16, Waggoner's body was found hanging from a tree. It looked like the rope had not broken Waggoner's neck but slowly strangled him.

Yes, Waggoner had a large horse herd, and he was a sharp trader in horseflesh, but there was no evidence that he stole horses. Several men were suspected in Waggoner's lynching, all association stock detectives, including possibly Frank Canton, Fred Coates, Joe Elliott, Mike Shonsey, Billy Lykins, and Tom Smith, but none of them were ever brought to trial. Later, Hiram Ijams, secretary of the Wyoming Stock Growers Association, said that Waggoner's name was on the association's death list.[7]

Next, the association set out to kill Johnson County homesteading rancher Nate Champion, an outspoken critic of the association. No evidence tied him to rustling, but the association believed that he had to be stealing cattle, nicknamed him "King of the Rustlers," and sent its men to kill him.[8]

Early on the morning of November 1, 1891, Canton, Coates, Elliott, Shonsey, and Lykins arrived at Champion's cabin to kill him. They burst through the door, ordering Champion to come with them. Champion, unable to recognize his attackers due to the sunlight coming through the door, reached for a pistol under his pillow and shot at them. They scrambled to get out of the way, but one of them, Billy Lykins, was hit, dying a month later.[9] As they were escaping, Champion recognized one of his attackers as association stock detective Joe Elliott.[10]

A few days later, Champion rode to nearby ranches, asking for assistance in finding his attackers. John Tisdale and another man, most likely Orley "Ranger" Jones, agreed to help. Searching Beaver Creek Canyon, they found a bloody tarp and other items, along with six horses, including one owned by Elliott. They then came upon association stock detective Mike Shonsey in the canyon.

Champion had had confrontations with Shonsey in the past, and he was certain that Shonsey was one of the men who had attacked him. Angrily threatening Shonsey, Champion demanded to know the names of the other attackers. Shonsey admitted who the would-be assassins were in front of Champion's companions: Joe Elliot, Frank Canton, Billy Lykins, and "Wood Box Jim."[11] John Tisdale and Ranger Jones were now available to testify in court that Elliott and others had attacked Champion.

On December 1, John Tisdale was returning to his ranch from Buffalo. His wagon was loaded with supplies and Christmas presents for his family. As he drove the wagon along the road, he was shot and killed. His murderer drove the wagon from the road and out of sight. He then shot the team of horses and Tisdale's dog.[12] Suspicion as to who did the shooting fell on Canton and Elliott, but no one was ever convicted of the murder.[13]

Two days after Tisdale's murder, Ranger Jones's body was found. He had been shot in the back and his body had been left in his wagon, which had been driven off the road and concealed. It was determined that Jones had been killed days before Tisdale. As with Tisdale, Jones's murderers were never determined.[14]

On February 8, 1892, the Johnson County District Court held a preliminary hearing on Elliott's attempt on Champion's life. Champion identified Elliott as one of his attackers, and Elliott was held in jail to await trial.[15]

Homesteading cattlemen formed the Northern Wyoming Farmers and Stock Growers' Association, announcing its own roundup, which would take place on May 1, 1892, one month before the Wyoming Stock Growers Association's regular roundup. They appointed Champion foreman and mocked the other association by calling themselves "Rustlers."[16]

The Wyoming Stock Growers Association had had enough; it was time to get rid of the rustlers. Association members especially worried that Elliott would break and identify them as the men behind the assassination attempt on Champion.

Association members met in the Cheyenne Club and began plotting to invade Johnson County to kill the rustlers and their supporters. Major Frank Wolcott and William "Billy" Irvine drafted invasion plans and would lead the invaders. One hundred association members contributed $1,000 each. Association stock detective Tom Smith traveled to Texas, where he hired twenty-six gunmen. Association members bought fifty-two horses in Colorado; they were concerned that if they bought that many horses in Wyoming, people would become suspicious. Other members bought supplies, including three freight wagons, guns, ammunition, and dynamite.[17]

Governor Amos Barber knew about and condoned the planned invasion. On March 23, he sent a telegram to Wyoming National Guard commanders ordering them to disobey any orders from county sheriffs. The invaders invited along with them Ed Towse, a reporter with the

The Johnson County invaders at Fort D. A. Russell, Cheyenne, Wyoming, on May 4, 1892. Some of the invaders are Tom Smith (no. 1), Major Frank Wolcott (13), William Irvine (15), Joe Elliott (17), Mike Shonsey (31), and Frank Canton (34).
COURTESY OF LOCAL HISTORY DEPARTMENT/JOHNSON COUNTY LIBRARY

Cheyenne Daily Leader who had told the cattlemen's side of Cattle Kate's hanging, and Sam Clover of the *Chicago Herald*. Clover promised to tell the association's version of the story to a national audience.

Everyone conveniently forgot Wyoming's recent state constitution, which some of the invaders had participated in drafting. Article 19 stated:

> *Section 6. Importing armed bodies to suppress violence prohibited; exception. No armed police force, or detective agency, or armed body, or unarmed body of men, shall ever be brought into this state, for the suppression of domestic violence, except upon the application of the legislature, or executive, when the legislature cannot be convened.*[18]

Frank Canton, association stock detective and former Johnson County sheriff, and others developed a death list naming seventy men to kill, including Johnson County sheriff W. E. "Red" Angus, his deputies, three county commissioners, and *Buffalo Bulletin* newspaper editor Joe DeBarthe.

Nineteen association conspirators met a chartered train from Denver, Colorado, that was carrying the supplies, horses, and twenty-six Texan gunmen, each promised $5 per day, expenses, a $3,000 accident policy, and $50 for every dead rustler. The train left Cheyenne on April 5, with fifty-two association members, association employees, Texan gunmen, and guests.[19]

At four o'clock in the morning, the invaders arrived in Casper, Wyoming, where they began their 150-mile ride north through a blizzard and gumbo mud to fulfill their murderous mission.

Following Wolcott's instructions, E. T. David, ranch manager for Senator Joseph Carey, cut the telegraph lines to Buffalo so that townspeople could not request help. As the invaders made their way through the blizzard toward Buffalo, Shonsey rode ahead to see whether he could obtain any new information. He returned to the invaders, informing them that Nate Champion was at the KC Ranch. Here was their chance to eliminate their nemesis. With Champion's death, the case against Elliott would evaporate and the cattle barons would remain protected. However, Canton argued that they were running out of time and should stick to their plan to attack Buffalo first. Major Wolcott and Billy Irvine wanted to attack the KC Ranch first. They finally put it to a vote of association members, who chose to attack the KC Ranch.

The invaders reached the KC Ranch along the Middle Fork of the Powder River on the night of April 8, taking positions in the ranch's barn and surrounding the cabin. Inside the cabin were Nate Champion, rancher Nick Ray, and Ben Jones and Billy Walker, two cowboys who were spending the night due to the storm.

The next morning, the storm cleared. Jones left the cabin carrying a bucket to the river. When he was out of sight of the cabin, he was quietly captured. Walker next came out of the cabin and walked behind the barn, where he was captured. Nick Ray stepped outside to see where Jones and Walker had gone. Major Wolcott nodded to D. E. "Texas Kid" Brooke, who fired a shot, striking Ray and signaling the rest of the invaders to open fire. Ray, knocked to the ground, started crawling to the cabin. Champion raced out, shooting at the assailants, got hold of Ray, and pulled him inside.

Nate Champion, second from the left, was named king of the rustlers by Wyoming cattle barons. COURTESY OF LOCAL HISTORY DEPARTMENT/JOHNSON COUNTY LIBRARY

Ray died later that morning as Champion put up a stiff defense, wounding three attackers. Champion kept a diary during the attack, writing, "They are still shooting and are all around the house. Boys, there is bullets coming in like hail."[20]

Jack Flagg and his stepson Alonzo Taylor rode by on the road to Buffalo. The invaders recognized Flagg as one of the men on the death list. They opened fire, and ten men chased the pair. The two eluded their pursuers and rode to Buffalo to sound the alarm.

Late in the day, the invaders pushed a burning wagon against the cabin. Champion wrote, "The house is all fired. Good bye boys, if I never see you again."[21] He escaped the flames, charging out of the cabin. Winchester in his left hand and pistol in his right, he reached a ravine but died there in a hail of bullets. Afterward, the invaders continued their advance toward Buffalo, but their siege at the KC Ranch had cost them precious time and the advantage of surprise.

Alerted by Flagg and Taylor, Sheriff Angus began organizing a posse. The "rustler" ranchers and townsmen rode out of Buffalo to confront the invaders. The posse's numbers would fluctuate over time, eventually growing to roughly four hundred men before the invasion was over.

As the invaders continued to advance on Buffalo, their scouts informed them that a large posse's camp was in front of them. Stock detectives Canton and Smith wanted to continue to Buffalo and fight it out, but the association members lost their nerve and didn't want to fight against aroused and armed ranchers and townsmen. The association members made the decision to retreat fourteen miles south of Buffalo to the TA Ranch on Crazy Woman Creek.

Texan Jim Dudley had been having trouble with horses. He was a heavyset man, and the horses couldn't handle his weight. He kept trading horses with other riders, trying to find one that could carry him. He mounted a new horse that immediately bucked him off, dislodging his Winchester and hurling it into the air. Hitting the ground, the Winchester fired, and the bullet hit Dudley's knee. Two cowboys drove Dudley in a spring wagon to Fort McKinney for medical care, where he later died from gangrene.[22]

Reaching the TA Ranch, the invaders fortified themselves in the ranch house and barn. In addition, they built a fortification on a nearby knoll using stockpiled timbers. When Sheriff Angus and his fifty-man posse reached the ranch, they surrounded the invaders and began digging their own fortifications. Sheriff Angus left the men there to watch the invaders and returned to Buffalo, gathered an additional forty men, and brought them back to the ranch. Early on the morning of April 11, back-and-forth firing between the posse and invaders developed. No one knows who started it, but the barrage became continuous. As word of the invasion spread through Johnson County, more men joined the posse surrounding the invaders.

Sherriff Angus again left for Buffalo. Posse members at the ranch elected Buffalo flour mill manager Arapaho Brown to lead them. Brown worked with Civil War veterans, directing the building of siege works to protect posse members as they slowly advanced toward the invaders.[23]

The invaders were desperate. They were running low on ammunition and food. There was no way they could fight their way out. They needed help. During the night, one invader sneaked through the posse's lines with a message. Riders carried his message one hundred miles to Douglas, Wyoming, where it was sent by telegram to Governor Amos Barber, who sent it to President Benjamin Harrison, requesting federal troops to quell the "insurrection." However, Harrison was sleeping, and no one dared wake him.

Barber then sent the telegram to Wyoming senators Frances E. Warren, an association member, and Joseph Carey, former association president. They went to the White House and woke President Harrison, who agreed to send troops to rescue the invaders. When Harrison's telegram reached Fort McKinney, the Sixth Cavalry set out on its rescue mission.

Meanwhile, back at the ranch, the posse captured the invaders' wagons and supplies, including ammunition and dynamite. Using one of the wagon's running gears and lumber, the men built a protective device that they named the "go-devil." They were advancing behind it to get within range of the barn and ranch house so that they could toss the invaders' own dynamite at them. The cavalry arrived just in time to aid the invaders. Colonel J. J. Van Horn negotiated with Sheriff Angus to allow the invaders to surrender to federal troops. Angus agreed, provided that the invaders would be handed over later to civilian authorities.

The troops marched the invaders to Fort McKinney and then escorted them to Cheyenne, where they were eventually released. The Texans hurried back to Texas. The cattle barons went back to business as usual. The state of Wyoming never brought charges against the invaders; Johnson County did, but the cattle barons' attorneys stalled in court until Johnson County ran out of public funds and had to drop the case.

In the end, no one was ever held accountable for the murders in Johnson County. Not only were the association members who planned and carried out the invasion responsible for the murders, but so were the governor, the senators, and every official who condoned the invasion or looked the other way.

DESPERATE TIMES CALL FOR DESPERATE MEASURES— KELLEN CUTSFORTH

When delving into the history of the Johnson County War, it is tempting to simply regurgitate the voluminous acts of violence committed on the Great Plains during one of the West's most infamous range wars. This is exactly what many author-historians do. These writers then attempt to decipher who fired the first shot. Instead of taking this well-worn approach, however, perhaps it is best to review the extenuating circumstances leading up to this epic conflict.

In the late nineteenth century, America's western frontier was quickly closing. Most of the open-range grazing land had fallen into the hands of wealthy ranchers and landowners. During Wyoming's infancy, as a territory and a state, most of its land was in the public domain, which meant that it was available to stock raising as an open range and as farmland for homesteading.[24]

Before the time of the Johnson County War (1889–1893), the state of Wyoming employed a stated principle of government policy known as prior appropriation to govern the use of these public lands. This doctrine related to water and land privileges, stating that Wyoming land and water rights were distributed to whoever settled the property first, and farmers and ranchers had to respect these boundaries.[25] It was first come, first served.

Also, prior to the range war, "roundups" occurred every spring to separate the cattle belonging to different ranches. A roundup entailed cowboys collecting stray and orphan calves, and then herding them back to the rightful owner's ranch. Often, branding of these orphan calves was done to show ownership by a specific rancher. In turn, ranchers generally allowed their cowboy employees to institute the practice of "taking mavericks" during a roundup.

Taking a maverick referred to the practice of stealing a lost, unbranded calf (or maverick) and keeping it for your own. Early on, a cowboy would brand the cattle with his employer's mark, return it to the herd, and receive a bonus of two and a half (or sometimes five) dollars a head for his honesty. But before long, cowboys found it more profitable to make their own brands and tattoo the maverick cattle, essentially making them their own, thus profiting from the larceny.[26]

Theft of maverick cattle was difficult to control on the immense open range, and ranchers usually instructed their cowboys to try to collect as many new calves as possible during the roundup, so losses to an outfit were never very significant. The maverick practice also allowed cowboys to improve their own lot by keeping some of the stray stock while most ranchers looked the other way.[27]

This mutually beneficial relationship helped maintain an uneasy truce between the wealthy landowners and the smaller ranchers in the area. It also proved especially useful in keeping the peace while the large ranching outfits consolidated their ownership by monopolizing large areas of the best land to prevent the bulk of the people entering Wyoming from laying claim to it. It is also important to note at this point that throughout the Great Plains and the late nineteenth century, this type of land manipulation was not uncommon and was certainly not unique to Wyoming. Nor was the practice ever illegal.

Furthermore, land disputes were not uncommon in the West, especially in connection with the Homestead Acts of the mid- and late nineteenth century. In the specific case of Johnson County, the major disputes between the smaller ranch settlers and the wealthy landowners did not erupt into a full-blown bloodbath until after the winter of 1886.

In November of that year, a local Wyoming newspaper, the *Big Horn Sentinel*, described one of the blizzards during the month as "a terror" and rife with "heavy snows of wind, snow and curses."[28] The winter raged on into 1887, delivering temperatures of forty to fifty degrees below zero, resulting in the deaths of entire herds of cattle.[29] The men on the range received no respite from the bludgeoning cold; several people perished during whiteouts and were not discovered until March.[30]

The storms were so severe that the *Cheyenne Daily Sun* described the devastation as "a year that is regarded as the most disastrous the territory has ever experienced."[31] The storms were even more catastrophic for the big ranchmen. It is estimated that large ranches lost nearly 50 percent of their cattle herds, and, accompanied by low market prices for beef at the time, most of these men were on the brink of utter ruin.[32] As further proof of the "exceedingly hard times," the Wyoming Stock Growers Association, which had a membership of 443 ranchers in 1886, saw its numbers plummet to only 183 members in 1888, and there was even talk of the organization going completely belly up.[33]

Platte Valley sheriff Malcolm Campbell also commented on the outcome of the severe storms, saying, "Then came the dread winter of 1886–7 which was to end all prosperity on the range and to lay the foundation for all the bitterness and bloody wrangling which occurred five years later."[34] By all accounts, the death toll was so severe that thousands of cattle perished and were piled up into every gulch. When the annual spring roundup took place, the yield was so poor that most cattle ranchers were contemplating not just a loss in profits but also a complete end to their ranching business.[35]

On the heels of these brutal blizzards came an extremely rare and intensely arid summer that swept over Wyoming like fire through a cane field. These two forms of weather phenomena, scorching summer and punishing winter, accompanied by a range that had been overstocked (mostly by small-time ranchers), depleted the grassland even further.[36] This deprivation caused a natural reaction by the large ranch owners to save their livelihood and keep their businesses afloat.

The landowners could no longer turn a blind eye to the "maverick" practice taking place, which was an act of theft. Charles B. Penrose, who was a doctor accompanying the Texas "invaders" during the range war, said of the rustling in Wyoming, "[In good times,] prosperous cattlemen could stand [rustling]. When, however, other causes diminished the profits of the cattle business, stealing became relatively of more account."[37] These facts are something not often discussed at length in many of the histories of the Johnson County War.

These "other causes," to use Penrose's term, relate to the horrendous winter that the cattlemen endured, which eventually forced these ranchers to lean on a law that was already on the books to help curtail mass rustling. The law was known as the Maverick Act. This act, passed in

1884, stated that all unbranded cattle in the open range automatically belonged to the cattlemen's association.[38] This push, however, did not stop the rustling, and by all accounts rustling continued at a greater pace.

The Wyoming Statutes of Crimes and Offenses, title 6, chapter 3, defines a *rustler* as "a person who steals, takes and carries, leads or drives away property of another with intent to deprive the owner or lawful possessor [and] is [therefore] guilty of larceny."[39] Simply put, a rustler is a damn dirty cow thief. And throughout this period, victims of rustling often remedied those thefts by prescribing a good dose of frontier justice to the criminals involved.

Many of the violent clashes during the Johnson County War can be attributed to the class conflict existing at the time between the established "ranchers" and the poorer "rustlers." Most historians rush to the defense of the rustlers because they often look to represent the working-class interests that lie with the bulk of the country's population. They paint the war as "a conflict between the few who had and were determined to keep and the many who wanted their fair share."[40] This attitude is a mythological stance that represents a moral ideological narrative used to prove a political point of view.

What should be stated outright at this point is that rustling of cattle and other livestock has always been illegal in the United States. In fact, the first "rustling laws" on the books in America date as far back as 1747, predating independence, and were adopted throughout the country's burgeoning states and territories. This was no different in Wyoming.

With that said, it would be ridiculous to try to justify the lynching of Ella "Cattle Kate" Watson and her husband Jim Averell at the hands of the cattlemen. But it would be just as ludicrous to try to defend the cold-blooded murder of range detective George Henderson, who, after the death of Cattle Kate, was hunted and viciously murdered in retaliation for the deaths of Watson and Averell. Most of the Johnson County War was tit for tat, revenge for a previous killing.

Did the cattlemen have the upper hand when it came to wealth and resources during the war? Yes, of course. But there is a reason why the opposing faction is commonly known as the "rustlers." Many of the people involved (though not all) were stealing cattle. They were taking mavericks from the range and using running brands to either alter brands or flat-out fire their own brands. This practice was frowned upon by the ranchers but allowed to continue because the losses were not catastrophic. Following the crushing consequences of the 1886–1887 winter, however, the ranchers could no longer afford the losses of orphan and stray calves. The cattle ranchers had the right to their property, the right to defend it, and the right to enforce a law that was already on the books for that very purpose.

In the years following the Johnson County War, some believed that the wealthy ranchers were in the right and sought justice by using frontier-style violence to defend what they regarded as their rights to land and water privileges. Others have seen the cattlemen as nothing more than robber barons murdering poor, unfortunate homesteaders just looking to make a living. Little, if any, of this is factual, just as some have suggested that the Jesse James gang was part of the rustlers' outfit or that legendary gunfighters Tom Horn and Big Nose George Parrot were somehow involved with the cattlemen. It's all trumped-up hogwash.

Even the first written "history" about the conflict falls into the realm of myth. Apparently, all copies of A. S. Mercer's *The Banditti of the Plains: Or the Cattlemen's Invasion of Wyoming in 1892* were confiscated and taken to the US courthouse in Denver to be destroyed in 1938. Only when some conscientious fellows got the janitor who was taking the volumes to the incinerator drunk were some of the books rescued, allowing the volume to survive to this day.[41] The tales surrounding the war become so goofy at points that they can be nothing less than pure fiction.

What is fact, however, is that due to catastrophic weather conditions, the years leading up to the Johnson County War were terrible for the ranchers. Furthermore, there was a significant but unmeasurable amount of rustling. When men are pushed to their limits in terms of retaining their livelihood, violence often results. So when deciding which side to take when it comes to the ranchers and rustlers, it is best to view the entire situation instead of focusing just on the violence.

ACKNOWLEDGMENTS

BILL AND KELLEN'S ACKNOWLEDGMENTS

A BIG THANK YOU TO CHRIS ENSS, LEADER OF THE MOST INTREPID Authors Posse, for her inspiration, guidance, and help throughout the process of crafting and marketing *Old West Showdown*. In fact, Chris helped develop the concept for this book. Thank you to Erin Turner and all the folks at TwoDot and Globe Pequot Press for believing in our storytelling abilities and giving us the opportunity to tell these tales.

Sherry Monahan and Monty McCord, fellow members of the Most Intrepid Authors Posse, thank you for your help and support in this endeavor. Thanks to Western Writers of America and its members, who provide constant support and encouragement. We most especially want to acknowledge and thank all those who have written books, magazine articles, and other documents and all those who have preserved documents to keep the memory of the Old West alive.

KELLEN'S ACKNOWLEDGMENTS

I would first like to thank my wife, Meghan, and my daughters, Cora and Vivian, who are a constant source of inspiration. Thank you to my parents, Allen and Patricia Cutsforth, for your constant support. I want to thank Dennis Hagen for reviewing this book and making much-needed corrections. I would also like to thank author Chris Enss for her personal guidance and influence on my writing career.

BILL'S ACKNOWLEDGMENTS

Phil "Theta" Bowden, thank you for your comprehensive critical review! Friends from the heart forever! Thanks to George Kush for providing information and your review of the defeat at the Little Bighorn chapter. Thanks to Jim Hatzell for his critique of the defeat at the Little Bighorn chapter. Thank you to the late Jim McLaird for providing your insights on Calamity Jane. Ed Madson, TA Ranch owner, thank you for your input on the Johnson County War. Dave Thompson, thanks for recommending that if I wanted a deeper look into Geronimo, I should read *Once They Moved Like the Wind* by David Roberts, and thanks for then loaning me your copy. Mike Pellerzi, thanks for your support and encouragement! Keep your powder dry! Ron Swift, thanks for your corrections! Robert Kean, thank you for your review of the gunfight at O.K. Corral and Calamity Jane chapters.

Thanks to my wife, Liz, for reviewing drafts, listening to me rant, and going on my crazy research trips with me. To my son, Chris; daughter, Becky; and son-in-law, Steve Wosick, thanks for your support. Thanks to my grandsons, Grant and Max, for bringing joy into our lives. Thanks to my mom, Gloria, and brother, Doug, for your support. Last but not least, thanks, Lord, for Your guidance and gifts to reason, write, and read. Thank You for my life, the good and the not so good.

NOTES

Chapter One

1. Steven Lubet, *Murder in Tombstone: The Forgotten Trial of Wyatt Earp* (New Haven, CT: Yale University Press, 2004), 288.
2. Ibid.
3. Casey Tefertiller, *Wyatt Earp: The Life Behind the Legend* (New York: John Wiley, 1997), 40–43.
4. Lubet, *Murder in Tombstone*, 288.
5. Tefertiller, *Wyatt Earp*, 76, 77.
6. Ibid.
7. Ibid., 113.
8. Ibid., 85.
9. Ibid., 113.
10. Albert Vetere Lannon, "134 Years Later—the Gunfight at the O.K. Corral," October 7, 2015, *Desert Times*, accessed January 23, 2017, www.tucsonlocalmedia.com/deserttimes/article_1d9faaec-6d11-11e5-943f-e7a9fb91172a.html.
11. Tefertiller, *Wyatt Earp*, 115.
12. Ibid.
13. Ibid., 116.
14. Casey Tefertiller and Jeff Morey, "O.K. Corral: A Gunfight Shrouded in Mystery," HistoryNet.com, accessed January 30, 2017, www.historynet.com/ok-corral.
15. Tefertiller, *Wyatt Earp*, 116.
16. Ibid., 118.
17. Ibid.
18. Ibid., 121.
19. The term *heeled* refers to being armed.
20. Alford E. Turner, *The O.K. Corral Inquest* (College Station, TX: Creative Publishing, 1981), 97.
21. Ibid., 98.
22. Ibid., 162.
23. Ibid., 204, 205.
24. Tefertiller, *Wyatt Earp*, 117, 118.
25. Ibid., 118.

26. Turner, *O.K. Corral Inquest*, 123.

27. Ibid., 55, 56.

28. Ibid., 45.

29. Joseph Clanton Transcript, Coroner's Inquest of the Gunfight at the OK Corral, Legal and Court History of Cochise County, Arizona Memory Project.

30. Turner, *O.K. Corral Inquest*, 136, 137.

31. Ibid.

32. Ibid., 137, 138.

33. Coleman Transcript, Coroner's Inquest of the Gunfight at the OK Corral, Legal and Court History of Cochise County, Arizona Memory Project.

34. King Transcript, Coroner's Inquest of the Gunfight at the OK Corral, Legal and Court History of Cochise County, Arizona Memory Project.

35. Turner, *O.K. Corral Inquest*, 138.

36. Ibid., 193.

37. Ibid., 146.

38. Ibid., 138, 139.

39. Ibid., 56.

40. Ibid., 138, 139.

41. Marshall Trimble, "What Was Doc Holliday's Weapon of Choice? And How Authentic Is the Crossdraw Rig Worn by Val Kilmer While Portraying the Doc in 1993's *Tombstone?*" *True West*, December 2, 2006.

42. Turner, *O.K. Corral Inquest*, 139.

43. Ibid., 71, 72.

44. Ibid., 76, 77.

45. Ibid., 93–95.

46. Tefertiller, *Wyatt Earp*, 124.

CHAPTER TWO

1. *The Northfield Bank Raid* (pamphlet; Northfield, MN: Northfield News, 2008; repr. from the *Northfield News*, 10th ed., August 27, September 3, 10, and 17, 1926), 19.

2. Thomas Coleman Younger, *The Story of Cole Younger, by Himself* (Saint Paul: Minnesota Historical Society, 2000), 75.

3. Mark Lee Gardner, *Shot All to Hell: Jesse James, the Northfield Raid, and the Wild West's Greatest Escape* (New York: HarperCollins, 2013), 215.

4. Ibid., 71.

5. Ibid., 77.

6. *Northfield Bank Raid*, 7.

7. Ibid.

8. Ibid., 7–8.

9. Gardner, *Shot All to Hell*, 79.

10. Ibid., 80.

11. Ibid., 89.

12. Ibid., 90.

13. Ibid., 91–92.

14. Ibid., 131.

15. Ted P. Yeatman, *Frank and Jesse James: The Story Behind the Legend* (Naperville, IL: Cumberland House, 2000), 30–35.

16. T. J. Stiles, *Jesse James: Last Rebel of the Civil War* (New York: Vintage Books, 2003), 88–90.

17. Ibid., 153–54.

18. Ibid., 210–11.

19. Ibid., 233–34.

20. Ibid., 251.

21. Ibid., 281–83.

22. Ibid., 289, 290.

23. Younger, *Story of Cole Younger*, 5.

24. Ibid., 6.

25. Ibid., 7.

26. Ibid., 9.

27. Stiles, *Jesse James*, 255, 256.

28. Gardner, *Shot All to Hell*, 36, 37.

29. Ibid., 37–39.

30. Ibid., 39–40.

31. Ibid., 23.

32. Stiles, *Jesse James*, 307–11, 322, 325.

33. Hans Louis Trefousse, *Ben Butler: The South Called Him Beast!* (New York: Twayne, 1957), 212.

34. Ibid., 111.

35. Ibid., 114.

36. Ibid., 123–24.

37. Ibid., 133.

38. Stiles, *Jesse James*, 324.

39. Yeatman, *Frank and Jesse James*, 344.

40. Dale L. Walker, *Legends and Lies: Great Mysteries of the American West* (New York: Tom Doherty, 1997), 88.

41. Ibid.

42. A. C. Stone, J. E. Starrs, and M. Stoneking, "Mitochondrial DNA Analysis of the Presumptive Remains of Jesse James," *Journal of Forensic Sciences* 46, no. 1 (2001): 173–76.

43. Stiles, *Jesse James*, 326–47.

44. Richard Slotkin, *Gunfighter Nation: The Myth of the Frontier in Twentieth-Century America* (Norman: University of Oklahoma Press, 1998), 128.

45. Eric J. Hobsbawm, *Primitive Rebels: Studies in Archaic Forms of Social Movement in the 19th and 20th Centuries* (New York: W. W. Norton, 1959), 13–29.

46. Stiles, *Jesse James*, 324–25.

47. Gardner, *Shot All to Hell*, 48, 49.

48. Ibid.
49. Ibid.
50. Ibid., 50.
51. Ibid., 50, 51.
52. Ibid., 51.
53. Ibid.
54. Ibid.
55. Ibid.
56. Ibid., 51.
57. Ibid., 52.
58. Ibid.
59. Ibid.
60. Ibid., 57.
61. Ibid., 52.

CHAPTER THREE

1. Joseph G. Rosa, *Wild Bill Hickok: The Man and His Myth* (Lawrence: University Press of Kansas, 1996), 236, 237.
2. J. W. Buel, *Heroes of the Plains* (Philadelphia: Historical Publishing, 1881), 44–48.
3. Rosa, *Wild Bill Hickok, Gunfighter: An Account of Hickok's Gunfights* (Norman: University of Oklahoma Press, 2003), 68, 69.
4. Rosa, *Wild Bill Hickok*, 217.
5. Joseph G. Rosa, *They Called Him Wild Bill: The Life and Adventures of James Butler Hickok* (Norman: University of Oklahoma Press, 1974), 4.
6. Elizabeth B. Custer, *Following the Guidon* (Norman: University of Oklahoma Press, 1966), 161.
7. Rosa, *They Called Him Wild Bill*, 16.
8. Ibid., 18, 22.
9. W. F. Cody, *Buffalo Bill's Life Story: An Autobiography* (New York: Cosmopolitan Book Corporation, 1920), 52.
10. Louis S. Warren, *Buffalo Bill's America: William Cody and the Wild West Show* (New York: Alfred A. Knopf, 2005), 62.
11. Rosa, *Wild Bill Hickok, Gunfighter*, 71.
12. James D. McLaird, *Wild Bill Hickok and Calamity Jane: Deadwood Legends* (Pierre: South Dakota State Historical Society Press, 2008), 8.
13. "Rock Creek Station State Historical Park," Fairbury.com, accessed May 12, 2017, www.fairbury.com/pages/history/rock_creek.html.
14. Rosa, *Wild Bill Hickok, Gunfighter*, 84.
15. Rosa, *Wild Bill Hickok, Gunfighter*, 69.
16. Ibid.
17. Ibid.
18. Ibid., 70.

19. Ibid.

20. Ibid., 70, 71.

21. "Border Tales—Life and Times of Wild Bill," manuscript draft, box 2, file folder 17, William Elsey Connelley Papers, WH905, Western History Collection, Denver Public Library.

22. Rosa, *Wild Bill Hickok, Gunfighter*, 77.

23. Ibid., 74.

24. "Border Tales," box 2, file folder 17, William Elsey Connelley Papers.

25. Ibid.

26. Rosa, *Wild Bill Hickok, Gunfighter*, 75.

27. Ibid.

28. "Border Tales," box 2, file folder 17, William Elsey Connelley Papers.

29. Rosa, *Wild Bill Hickok, Gunfighter*, 74 and 75.

30. "Border Tales," box 2, file folder 17, William Elsey Connelley Papers.

31. Ibid.

32. Rosa, *Wild Bill Hickok, Gunfighter*, 75.

33. Ibid., 76.

34. Ibid.

35. Ibid., 71.

36. Ibid., 75.

37. Ibid., 76.

38. Ibid., 75.

39. Ibid., 76.

40. Ibid., 77.

41. Ibid.

42. Ibid., 78.

43. Ibid., 79.

44. Ibid., 68.

45. Mark Dugan, *Tales Never Told around the Campfire: True Stories of the American Frontier* (Athens: Swallow Press/Ohio University Press, 1992), 32, 33.

46. Ibid., 30, 31, 34, 40.

47. Ibid., 40, 41.

48. William Monroe McCanles, "The Only Living Eye Witness," *Nebraska Historical Magazine* 10, no. 2 (April–June 1927): 47.

49. Dugan, *Tales Never Told*, 40, 41.

50. Ibid., 41, 43, 44.

51. Ibid., 43, 44.

52. Charles Dawson, *Pioneer Tales of the Oregon Trail and of Jefferson County* (Topeka, KS: Topeka, Crane, 1912), 203, 204.

53. Dugan, *Tales Never Told*, 47.

54. Ibid., 48, 49.

55. Ibid., 49.

56. Ibid.

57. Dawson, *Pioneer Tales*, 215.

58. Rosa, *Wild Bill Hickok, Gunfighter*, 74, 75.
59. McCanles, "Only Living Eye Witness," 48.
60. Dugan, *Tales Never Told*, 44, 45.
61. Ibid., 49.
62. Ibid., 51.
63. McCanles, "Only Living Eye Witness," 48.
64. Ibid.
65. Dugan, *Tales Never Told*, 53.
66. McCanles, "Only Living Eye Witness," 48.
67. Ibid.
68. Dugan, *Tales Never Told*, 53.
69. McCanles, "Only Living Eye Witness," 49.
70. Dugan, *Tales Never Told*, 53.
71. Dawson, *Pioneer Tales*, 219, 220.
72. Dugan, *Tales Never Told*, 53, 54.
73. Ibid., 54.
74. Ibid., 55.
75. Rosa, *Wild Bill Hickok: The Man*, 233.

CHAPTER FOUR

1. James D. McLaird, *Calamity Jane: The Woman and the Legend* (Norman: University of Oklahoma Press, 2005), 17.
2. Horatio Maguire, *Black Hills Wonderland* (Chicago: Donnelley, Lloyd, 1877), 304.
3. Richard W. Etulain, *Calamity Jane: A Reader's Guide* (Norman: University of Oklahoma Press, 2015), 9.
4. McLaird, *Calamity Jane*, 18.
5. Martha Canary, *Life and Adventures of Calamity Jane by Herself* (Fairfield, WA: Ye Galleon Press, 1979), 1.
6. McLaird, *Calamity Jane*, 22.
7. Ibid.
8. Canary, *Life and Adventures*, 1.
9. McLaird, *Calamity Jane*, 34.
10. Ibid.
11. Ibid., 22.
12. Etulain, *Calamity Jane*, 6–7.
13. McLaird, *Calamity Jane*, 49.
14. Ibid.
15. Etulain, *Calamity Jane*, 6–7.
16. McLaird, *Calamity Jane*, 49.
17. Ibid., 46.
18. Etulain, *Calamity Jane*, 8.
19. McLaird, *Calamity Jane*, 55.

20. Ibid., 56.
21. Canary, *Life and Adventures*, 3.
22. McLaird, *Calamity Jane*, 32–33.
23. Frank J. Wilstach, *Wild Bill Hickok: The Prince of Pistoleers* (New York: Doubleday, Page, 1926), 264–65.
24. Canary, *Life and Adventures*, 4–5.
25. Harry Young, *Hard Knocks: A Life of the Vanishing West* (Portland, OR: J. K. Gill, 1915), 221.
26. Joseph Foster Anderson, *I Buried Hickok: The Memoirs of White Eye Anderson*, ed. William B. Secrest (College Station, TX: Creative Publishing, 1980), 120.
27. Young, *Hard Knocks*, 211–12.
28. Anderson, *I Buried Hickok*, 93.
29. Richard B. Hughes, *Pioneer Years in the Black Hills* (Rapid City, SD: Dakota Alpha Press, 2002), 125.
30. Anderson, *I Buried Hickok*, 121.
31. Canary, *Life and Adventures*, 4.
32. McLaird, *Calamity Jane*, 212–13.
33. Helen Rezatto, *Mount Moriah: The Story of Deadwood's Boot Hill* (Rapid City, SD: Fenwyn Press, 1989), 71.
34. Etulain, *Calamity Jane*, 19, 94–95, 146–47.
35. James McLaird, personal email communication to Bill Markley, March 28, 2017.
36. Canary, *Life and Adventures*, 5.
37. Agnes Wright Spring, *The Cheyenne and Black Hills Stage and Express Routes* (Lincoln: University of Nebraska Press, 1967), 189–92.
38. Dora DuFran [d'Dée, pseud.], *Low Down on Calamity Jane* (Rapid City, SD: N.p., 1932), 10.

Chapter Five

1. Fredrick Whittaker, *A Popular Life of Gen. George A. Custer* (New York: Sheldon, 1876), 391; italics in original.
2. Ronald Hamilton Nichols, *In Custer's Shadow: Major Marcus Reno* (Norman: University of Oklahoma Press, 1999), 85.
3. James Donovan, *A Terrible Glory: Custer and the Little Bighorn—the Last Great Battle of the American West* (New York: Back Bay Books, 2008), 93.
4. Nichols, *In Custer's Shadow*, 141.
5. Donovan, *Terrible Glory*, 162–68.
6. Marcus A. Reno and United States Army Courts of Inquiry, *The Official Record of a Court of Inquiry Convened at Chicago, Illinois, January 13, 1879, by the President of the United States upon the Request of Major Marcus A. Reno, 7th U.S. Cavalry, to Investigate His Conduct at the Battle of the Little Big Horn, June 25–26, 1876* (Pacific Palisades, CA: W. A. Graham, 1951), 521, http://digicoll.library.wisc.edu/cgi-bin/History/History-idx?id=History.Reno.

7. Donovan, *Terrible Glory*, 56.

8. Evan S. Connell, *Son of the Morning Star: Custer and the Little Bighorn* (New York: Harper and Row, 1984), 197.

9. Kenneth Hammer, ed., *Custer in '76: Walter Camp's Notes on the Custer Fight* (Norman: University of Oklahoma Press, 1990), 247.

10. Alfred H. Terry, *The Field Diary of General Alfred H. Terry: The Yellowstone Expedition—1876*, 2nd ed. (Bellevue, NE: Old Army Press, 1970), 4, 5.

11. Donovan, *Terrible Glory*, 212.

12. Ibid., 209, 210.

13. Ibid., 213.

14. Ibid., 214, 215.

15. Hammer, *Custer in '76*, 84.

16. Ibid., 216.

17. Donovan, *Terrible Glory*, 221.

18. Hammer, *Custer in '76*, 232.

19. General Charles M. Roe to Dr. John M. Cooke, April 22, 1906, J. M. Cooke papers, private collection.

20. Donovan, *Terrible Glory*, 243.

21. Hammer, *Custer in '76*, 92–94.

22. Donovan, *Terrible Glory*, 255.

23. John M Carroll, ed., *The Gibson-Edgerly Narrative* (Byron, TX: Private printing, 1977), 5.

24. Captain Thomas B. Weir to Dr. A. H. Cooke, October 22, 1876, W. W. Cooke papers, private collection.

25. W. A. Graham, *The Story of the Little Big Horn: Custer's Last Fight* (Harrisburg, PA: Stackpole, 1959), 53.

26. Donovan, *Terrible Glory*, 256.

27. Hammer, *Custer in '76*, 93.

28. Donovan, *Terrible Glory*, 256.

29. Graham, *Story of the Little Big Horn*, 54.

30. Donovan, *Terrible Glory*, 257–59.

31. Cyrus Townsend Brady, *Indian Fights and Fighters* (Lincoln: University of Nebraska Press, 1971), 404.

32. Jeffry D. Wert, *Custer: The Controversial Life of George Armstrong Custer* (New York: Touchstone, 1996), 348.

33. Hammer, *Custer in '76*, 55, 56.

34. Ibid., 70.

35. Ibid., 56.

36. Connell, *Son of the Morning Star*, 30.

37. Brady, *Indian Fights and Fighters*, 399.

38. Paul Andrew Hutton, ed., *The Custer Reader* (Lincoln: University of Nebraska Press, 1992), 317.

39. Richard A. Roberts, *Reminiscences of General Custer: Custer's Last Battle* (Monroe, MI: Monroe County Library, 1978), 26.

40. Nelson A. Miles, *Personal Recollections and Observations of General Nelson A. Miles* (Chicago: Werner, 1896), 290.

41. George Kush, personal communication to Bill Markley, April 28, 2017.

42. Dale L. Walker, *Legends and Lies: Great Mysteries of the American West* (New York: Tom Doherty, 1997), 232.

43. T. J. Stiles, *Custer's Trials: A Life on the Frontier of a New America* (New York: Alfred A. Knopf, 2015), 4.

44. Stiles, *Custer's Trials*, xvi.

45. Stiles, *Custer's Trials*, 27.

46. Walker, *Legends and Lies*, 232.

47. Stiles, *Custer's Trials*, 98, 99.

48. Ibid., 101.

49. Ibid., 100.

50. Ibid., 102, 103.

51. Robert M. Utley, *Cavalier in Buckskin: George Armstrong Custer and the Western Military Frontier*, rev. ed. (Norman: University of Oklahoma Press, 2001), 107.

52. Bill Thayer, "George A. Custer," Bill Thayer's website, accessed April 29, 2017, http://penelope.uchicago.edu/Thayer/E/Gazetteer/Places/America/United_States/Army/USMA/Cullums_Register/1966*.html.

53. Donovan, *Terrible Glory*, 63.

54. Ibid.

55. Ibid., 64.

56. Ibid.

57. Ibid.

58. Walker, *Legends and Lies*, 233.

59. Donovan, *Terrible Glory*, 175, 176.

60. Connell, *Son of the Morning Star*, 257.

61. Robert Nightengale, "Battle of Little Bighorn Coverup," HistoryNet.com, accessed August 22, 2017, www.historynet.com/battle-of-little-bighorn.

62. Donovan, *Terrible Glory*, 213.

63. Reno and United States Army Courts of Inquiry, *Official Record of a Court of Inquiry*, 35.

64. Interview notes, box 1, file folder 57, Robert S. Ellison, Walter M. Camp Papers, WH1702, Western History Collection, Denver Public Library.

Chapter Six

1. Glenn Danford Bradley, *The Story of the Pony Express* (Chicago: A. C. McClurg, 1913), 9.

2. Steve Friesen, *Buffalo Bill: Scout, Showman, Visionary* (Golden, CO: Fulcrum, 2010), 7.

3. Alexander Majors, *Seventy Years on the Frontier* (Minneapolis: Ross and Haines, 1965), 176–77.

4. Friesen, *Buffalo Bill*, 7.

5. Ibid., 15.

6. Ibid., 16.

7. Ibid.

8. R. L. Wilson, *Buffalo Bill's Wild West: An American Legend* (New York: Random House, 1998), 316.

9. Ibid.

10. Jeff Broome, "Death at Summit Springs: Susanna Alderdice and the Cheyennes," HistoryNet.com, accessed March 13, 2017, www.historynet.com/death-at-summit -springs-susanna-alderdice-and-the-cheyennes.htm.

11. Friesen, *Buffalo Bill*, 20.

12. Broome, "Death at Summit Springs."

13. Don Russell, *The Lives and Legends of Buffalo Bill* (Norman: University of Oklahoma Press, 1972), 133, 138, 147.

14. Friesen, *Buffalo Bill*, 17.

15. Kellen Cutsforth, "Evelyn Booth Took a Shot at Fame as a Partner of Buffalo Bill's Wild West: But Cody's English Benefactor Is Largely Forgotten Today," *Wild West* 26 (2014): 29.

16. "American Exhibition," Wikipedia, accessed March 14, 2017, https://en.wikipedia .org/wiki/American_Exhibition#cite_note-considered-4.

17. Louis S. Warren, *Buffalo Bill's America: William Cody and the Wild West Show* (New York: Alfred A. Knopf, 2005), 283.

18. Cutsforth, "Evelyn Booth," 29.

19. Show program, box 2, William Frederick Cody/Buffalo Bill Papers, WH72, Western History Collection, Denver Public Library.

20. Wilson, *Buffalo Bill's Wild West*, 316.

21. Deanne Stillman, *Blood Brothers: The Story of the Strange Friendship between Sitting Bull and Buffalo Bill* (New York: Simon and Schuster, 2017), xiii.

22. Steve Friesen, "The Man Behind the Legend," *American Cowboy*, collector's ed., 2012/2013, 54.

23. Warren, *Buffalo Bill's America*, ix.

24. W. F. Cody, *Buffalo Bill's Life Story: An Autobiography* (New York: Cosmopolitan Book Corporation, 1920), 47–48.

25. Friesen, *Buffalo Bill*, 4, 7.

26. Warren, *Buffalo Bill's America*, 19, 20.

27. Ibid., 20.

28. Ibid., 79.

29. Cody, *Buffalo Bill's Life Story*, 190–91.

30. William F. Cody, *The Life of Hon. William F. Cody, Known as Buffalo Bill, the Famous Hunter, Scout and Guide: An Autobiography* (Hartford, CT: F. E. Bliss, 1879), 260, 261.

31. Warren, *Buffalo Bill's America*, 112.

32. Paul L. Hedren, *First Scalp for Custer: The Skirmish at Warbonnet Creek, Nebraska, July 17, 1876* (Lincoln: Nebraska State Historical Society, 2005), 23–25.

33. Friesen, *Buffalo Bill*, 38.

34. Cody, *Life of Hon. William F. Cody*, 343, 344.

35. Bobby Bridger, *Buffalo Bill and Sitting Bull: Inventing the West* (Austin: University of Texas Press, 2002), 256.

36. Warren, *Buffalo Bill's America*, 119.

37. Hedren, *First Scalp for Custer*, 28–38.

38. Cody, *Buffalo Bill's Life Story*, 265.

39. Friesen, *Buffalo Bill*, 119–22.

40. Bridger, *Buffalo Bill and Sitting Bull*, 428–30.

41. Robert E. Bonner, *William F. Cody's Wyoming Empire: The Buffalo Bill Nobody Knows* (Norman: University of Oklahoma Press, 2007), 53.

42. Bridger, *Buffalo Bill and Sitting Bull*, 440–41.

43. Ibid., 443.

CHAPTER SEVEN

1. Joseph M. Marshall III, *The Journey of Crazy Horse: A Lakota History* (New York: Penguin Books, 2004), xxi.

2. Marshall, *Journey of Crazy Horse*, 3, 4, 19.

3. Douglas C. McChristian, *Fort Laramie: Military Bastion of the High Plains* (Norman, OK: Arthur H. Clark, 2008), 59.

4. Mari Sandoz, *Crazy Horse: The Strange Man of the Oglalas*, 50th anniversary ed. (Lincoln: University of Nebraska Press, 1961), 117, 118.

5. Edward Clown Family, as told to William B. Matson, *Crazy Horse: The Warrior's Life and Legacy* (Layton, UT: Gibbs Smith, 2016), 70.

6. Marc H. Abrams, *Sioux War Dispatches: Reports from the Field, 1876–1877* (Yardley, PA: Westholme, 2012), 325, 326.

7. Kingsley M. Bray, "Crazy Horse Genealogy," American-Tribes.com, accessed May 17, 2017, www.american-tribes.com/Lakota/BIO/CrazyHorse.htm.

8. Thomas Powers, *The Killing of Crazy Horse* (New York: Alfred A. Knopf, 2010), 275, 276.

9. Paul L. Hedren, *After Custer: Loss and Transformation in Sioux Country* (Norman: University of Oklahoma Press, 2011), 144.

10. Jesse M. Lee, "The Capture and Death of an Indian Chieftain," *Journal of the Military Service Institution of the United States*, May–June 1914, 326, 327.

11. Candy Moulton, *Valentine T. McGillycuddy: Army Surgeon, Agent to the Sioux*, Western Frontiersmen (Norman, OK: Arthur H. Clark, 2011), 124.

12. Ibid., 124–25.

13. Ibid., 125.

14. Powers, *Killing of Crazy Horse*, 360.

15. Lee, "Capture and Death of an Indian Chieftain," 328.

16. Hedren, *After Custer*, 144.

17. Powers, *Killing of Crazy Horse*, 370.

18. Lee, "Capture and Death of an Indian Chieftain," 330.
19. Powers, *Killing of Crazy Horse*, 371.
20. Ibid.
21. Hedren, *After Custer*, 145.
22. Powers, *Killing of Crazy Horse*, 374, 375.
23. Moulton, *Valentine T. McGillycuddy*, 127–29.
24. Powers, *Killing of Crazy Horse*, 376–78.
25. Ibid., 379–80.
26. Lee, "Capture and Death of an Indian Chieftain," 339.
27. John G. Bourke, *On the Border with Crook* (New York: Skyhorse, 2014), 421.
28. Lee, "Capture and Death of an Indian Chieftain," 333–34.
29. Hedren, *After Custer*, 145, 146.
30. Powers, *Killing of Crazy Horse*, 195, 407.
31. Ibid., 407, 408.
32. Ibid., 408–10.
33. Ibid., 411–12.
34. Lee, "Capture and Death of an Indian Chieftain," 338.
35. Powers, *Killing of Crazy Horse*, 412.
36. Ibid., 426.
37. Ibid.
38. E. A. Brininstool, *Crazy Horse: The Invincible Ogalalla Sioux Chief* (Los Angeles: Wetzel, 1949), 47; italics in the original.
39. Dale L. Walker, *Legends and Lies: Great Mysteries of the American West* (New York: Tom Doherty, 1997), 276.
40. Ibid.
41. Ibid., 283.
42. Ibid., 286.
43. Box 3, envelope 1, galley proof for Eleanor H. Hinman interviews on the life and death of Crazy Horse, M108, Western History Collection, Denver Public Library.
44. Walker, *Legends and Lies*, 285.
45. Ibid., 286.
46. Ibid.
47. Ibid., 287.
48. Box 3, envelope 1, galley proof for Eleanor H. Hinman interviews.
49. Walker, *Legends and Lies*, 287.
50. Ibid.
51. Ibid.
52. Ibid., 288.
53. Ibid., 289.
54. Ibid.
55. Ibid.
56. Ibid.
57. Ibid.
58. Ibid., 290.

59. Ibid.
60. Ibid., 291.
61. Ibid.
62. Ibid.
63. Ibid., 292.
64. Ibid.
65. Ibid.
66. Sandoz, *Crazy Horse*, 407.
67. Ibid.
68. Ibid.
69. Ibid.
70. Ibid.
71. Ibid., 408.
72. Ibid.
73. Box 3, envelope 1, galley proof for Eleanor H. Hinman interviews.

CHAPTER EIGHT

1. Robert M. Utley, *Billy the Kid: A Short and Violent Life* (Lincoln: University of Nebraska Press, 1989), 184.
2. Pat Garrett, *The Authentic Life of Billy, the Kid* (Santa Fe: New Mexican Printing and Publishing, 1882), 145.
3. Utley, *Billy the Kid*, 190, 191.
4. Garrett, *Authentic Life of Billy*, 150.
5. Mark Lee Gardner, *To Hell on a Fast Horse: Billy the Kid, Pat Garrett, and the Epic Chase to Justice in the Old West* (New York: HarperCollins, 2010), 169, 170.
6. Ibid., 170.
7. Garrett, *Authentic Life of Billy*, 151, 152.
8. Utley, *Billy the Kid*, 194.
9. Gardner, *To Hell on a Fast Horse*, 173, 174.
10. Ibid., 174.
11. Ibid., 178.
12. Ibid., 175.
13. W. C. Jameson, *Billy the Kid: Beyond the Grave* (Lanham, MD: Taylor Trade, 2005), 15.
14. Ibid., 23.
15. Ibid., 126.
16. Gardner, *To Hell on a Fast Horse*, 254.
17. Jameson, *Billy the Kid*, 141, 142.
18. Garrett, *Authentic Life of Billy*, 154.
19. Keith Coffman, "Rare Billy the Kid Photograph Sold for $2.3 Million," Reuters, June 27, 2011, accessed April 15, 2017, www.reuters.com/article/us-auction-billykid -photo-idUSTRE75O1HX20110627.

20. Dale L. Walker, *Legends and Lies: Great Mysteries of the American West* (New York: Tom Doherty, 1997), 122.

21. Kathy Weiser, "Old West Legends: John William Poe—Hunting Billy the Kid," Legends of America, accessed April 15, 2017, www.legendsofamerica.com/law-johnpoe .html.

22. Walker, *Legends and Lies*, 123.

23. Gardner, *To Hell on a Fast Horse*, 168.

24. Ibid.

25. Newspaper clippings, "Billy the Kid" or Bonney, William H., vertical file, Western History Collection, Denver Public Library.

26. Gardner, *To Hell on a Fast Horse*, 171.

27. Jameson, *Billy the Kid*, 61.

28. Walker, *Legends and Lies*, 123.

29. Ibid.

30. Jameson, *Billy the Kid*, 62.

31. Ibid., 109.

32. Ibid., 64.

33. Jon Tuska, *Billy the Kid: A Handbook* (Lincoln: University of Nebraska Press, 1983), 125.

34. Jameson, *Billy the Kid*, 64.

35. Ibid., 66.

36. Ibid.

37. Ibid., 2.

38. Ibid., 2, 3.

39. Ibid., 25, 26.

40. Ibid., 108–10.

41. "Governor Mabry Pins Imposter Tag on 'Billy the Kid,'" *Rocky Mountain News*, November 30, 1950.

42. Jameson, *Billy the Kid*, 108–10.

43. Ibid., 105.

CHAPTER NINE

1. Anton Treuer, *The Indian Wars: Battles, Bloodshed, and the Fight for Freedom on the American Frontier* (Washington, DC: National Geographic Partners, 2016), 269.

2. Ibid.

3. Peter Newark, *The Illustrated Encyclopedia of the Old West* (London: Brockhampton Press, 1998), 105.

4. Ibid.

5. Newark, *Illustrated Encyclopedia*, 107.

6. Treuer, *Indian Wars*, 269.

7. Ibid.

8. Ibid.

9. Newark, *Illustrated Encyclopedia*, 107.

10. Treuer, *Indian Wars*, 270.

11. Ibid.

12. Treuer, *Indian Wars*, 271.

13. David Roberts, *Once They Moved Like the Wind: Cochise, Geronimo and the Apache Wars* (New York: Simon and Schuster, 1993), 15.

14. Ibid., 112.

15. Ibid., 112, 113.

16. Ibid., 116.

17. Ibid., 115.

18. Ibid., 118.

19. Ibid., 120.

20. Edwin R. Sweeney, *Cochise: Chiricahua Apache Chief* (Norman: University of Oklahoma Press, 1991), 144–46.

21. Roberts, *Once They Moved Like the Wind*, 22–23.

22. Sweeney, *Cochise*, 152.

23. Steve Ayers, *Camp Verde* (Mount Pleasant, SC: Arcadia, 2010), 17.

24. *Merriam-Webster*, s.v. "terrorism (*n.*)," www.merriam-webster.com/dictionary/terrorism.

25. Roberts, *Once They Moved Like the Wind*, 209.

26. Ibid.

27. Ibid., 210.

28. Ibid.

29. Ibid., 210–11.

30. Ibid., 251.

31. Ibid., 251–52.

32. Paul Andrew Hutton, "Was Geronimo a Terrorist? Tracing America's View of the Apache Warrior from Bloodthirsty Terrorist to Patriot Chief," *True West*, July 28, 2011, https://truewestmagazine.com/was-geronimo-a-terrorist/.

33. Guy Adams, "The Big Question: Who Was Geronimo, and Why Is There Controversy over His Remains?" *Independent*, June 22, 2009, www.independent.co.uk/news/world/americas/the-big-question-who-was-geronimo-and-why-is-there-controversy-over-his-remains-1714167.html.

34. Roberts, *Once They Moved Like the Wind*, 62, 63.

35. Robert M. Utley, *Geronimo* (New Haven, CT: Yale University Press, 2012), 10.

36. S. M. Barrett, *Geronimo, His Own Story: The Autobiography of a Great Patriot Warrior*, ed. Fredrick W. Turner III (New York: Ballantine Books, 1970), 81, 82.

37. Ibid., 84.

38. Utley, *Geronimo*, 26–28.

39. Paul Andrew Hutton, *The Apache Wars: The Hunt for Geronimo, the Apache Kid, and the Captive Boy Who Started the Longest War in American History* (New York: Broadway Books, 2016), 174, 182–85.

40. Barrett, *Geronimo, His Own Story*, 140.

41. Roberts, *Once They Moved Like the Wind*, 155–57.

42. Ibid., 161–70.
43. Ibid., 202.
44. Dee Brown, *Bury My Heart at Wounded Knee: An Indian History of the American West* (New York: Henry Holt, 2001), 402–7.
45. Ibid., 408.
46. Ibid., 410, 421.
47. Edwin R. Sweeney, *From Cochise to Geronimo: The Chiricahua Apaches, 1874–1889* (Norman: University of Oklahoma Press, 2010), 572.
48. Roberts, *Once They Moved Like the Wind*, 299, 300.
49. Barrett, *Geronimo, His Own Story*, 184.

CHAPTER TEN

1. Stephen E. Ambrose, *Nothing Like It in the World: The Men Who Built the Transcontinental Railroad, 1863–1869* (New York: Simon and Schuster, 2000), 220.
2. "Wyoming Stock Growers Association: Guardians of Wyoming's Cow Country Since 1872," Wyoming Stock Growers Association website, accessed April 4, 2017, www.wysga.org/aboutwsga.aspx.
3. Paul Trachtman, *The Gunfighters*, The Old West (Alexandria, VA: Time-Life Books, 1974), 206.
4. Earl Madsen, personal email communication to Bill Markley, February 21, 2016.
5. Ibid.
6. Larry K. Brown, *Coyotes and Canaries: Characters Who Made the West Wild . . . and Wonderful!* (Glendo, WY: High Plains Press, 2002), 65–69.
7. Mark Boardman, "Wave of Violence: The Lynching of Tom Waggoner Marked the Start of the Johnson County War," *True West*, June 2016, 12.
8. John W. Davis, *Wyoming Range War: The Infamous Invasion of Johnson County* (Norman: University of Oklahoma Press, 2010), 99.
9. Ibid., 101–2.
10. Ibid., 124.
11. Ibid., 104.
12. Ibid., 109.
13. Ibid., 115.
14. Ibid., 111.
15. Ibid., 124.
16. Ibid., 140.
17. Trachtman, *Gunfighters*, 208, 209.
18. Max Maxfield, *Constitution of the State of Wyoming*, November 12, 2008, Wyoming Secretary of State website, accessed April 5, 2017, https://soswy.state.wy.us/Forms/Publications/09WYConstitution.pdf.
19. Trachtman, *Gunfighters*, 209, 210.
20. Davis, *Wyoming Range War*, 285.
21. Ibid., 286.
22. Ibid., 157, 160, 193.

23. Ibid., 164–65.

24. "Johnson County War," Wikipedia, accessed March 28, 2017, https://en.wikipedia.org/wiki/Johnson_County_War.

25. Kathy Weiser, "Wyoming Legends: Johnson County War," Legends of America, accessed March 27, 2017, www.legendsofamerica.com/wy-johnsoncountywar.html.

26. Charles B. Penrose, *The Rustler Business* (Douglas, WY: Douglas Budget, 1959), 8.

27. Ibid.

28. Davis, *Range War*, 33.

29. Nathaniel Burt, *Compass American Guides: Wyoming*, 3rd ed. (New York: Compass American Guides, 1998), 156.

30. Davis, *Wyoming Range War*, 34.

31. Ibid.

32. Ibid., 35.

33. Ibid.

34. Robert B. David, *Malcolm Campbell, Sheriff* (Casper, WY: Wyomingana, 1932), 123.

35. David, *Malcolm Campbell, Sheriff*, 123–24.

36. Burton, *Compass American Guides: Wyoming*, 156.

37. Penrose, *Rustler Business*, 7.

38. Jeremy Agnew, *The Old West in Fact and Film: History versus Hollywood* (Jefferson, NC: McFarland, 2012), 40.

39. Wyoming Statutes, § 6-4-413 (2014), "Rustling; penalty," Justia, accessed April 1, 2017, http://law.justia.com/codes/wyoming/2014/title-6/chapter-3/article-4/section-6-3-413.

40. Helena Huntington Smith, prologue to *The War on Powder River* (New York: McGraw-Hill, 1966), xii.

41. Letter, box 12, envelope 1, Pershing, James H., Papers, -M611, Denver Public Library.

BIBLIOGRAPHY

MANUSCRIPTS AND PRIMARY RESOURCES

Bonney, William H., or "Billy the Kid." Vertical file. Western History Collection. Denver Public Library.

Connelley, William Elsey. Papers. Western History Collection. Denver Public Library.

Cooke, J. M. Papers. Private collection.

Cooke, W. W. Papers. Private collection.

Ellison, Robert S., and Walter M. Camp. Papers. Western History Collection. Denver Public Library.

Hinman, Eleanor H. Interviews on the life and death of Crazy Horse. Western History Collection. Denver Public Library.

Legal and Court History of Cochise County. Arizona Memory Project.

Pershing, James H. Papers. Western History Collection. Denver Public Library.

Reno, Marcus A., and United States Army Courts of Inquiry. *The Official Record of a Court of Inquiry Convened at Chicago, Illinois, January 13, 1879, by the President of the United States upon the Request of Major Marcus A. Reno, 7th U.S. Cavalry, to Investigate His Conduct at the Battle of the Little Big Horn, June 25–26, 1876.* Pacific Palisades, CA: W. A. Graham, 1951. http://digicoll.library.wisc.edu/cgi-bin/History/History-idx?id=History.Reno.

BOOKS

Abrams, Marc H. *Sioux War Dispatches: Reports from the Field, 1876–1877.* Yardley, PA: Westholme, 2012.

Agnew, Jeremy. *The Old West in Fact and Film: History versus Hollywood.* Jefferson, NC: McFarland, 2012.

Ambrose, Stephen E. *Nothing Like It in the World: The Men Who Built the Transcontinental Railroad, 1863–1869.* New York: Simon and Schuster, 2000.

Anderson, Joseph Foster. *I Buried Hickok: The Memoirs of White Eye Anderson.* Edited by William B. Secrest. College Station, TX: Creative Publishing, 1980.

Ayers, Steve. *Camp Verde.* Mount Pleasant, SC: Arcadia, 2010.

Barrett, S. M. *Geronimo, His Own Story: The Autobiography of a Great Patriot Warrior.* Edited by Fredrick W. Turner III. New York: Ballantine Books, 1970.

Bonner, Robert E. *William F. Cody's Wyoming Empire: The Buffalo Bill Nobody Knows.* Norman: University of Oklahoma Press, 2007.

Bourke, John G. *On the Border with Crook.* New York: Skyhorse, 2014.

Bradley, Glenn Danford. *The Story of the Pony Express.* Chicago: A. C. McClurg, 1913.

Brady, Cyrus Townsend. *Indian Fights and Fighters.* Lincoln: University of Nebraska Press, 1971.

Bridger, Bobby. *Buffalo Bill and Sitting Bull: Inventing the West.* Austin: University of Texas Press, 2002.

Brininstool, E. A. *Crazy Horse: The Invincible Ogalalla Sioux Chief.* Los Angeles: Wetzel, 1949.

Brown, Dee. *Bury My Heart at Wounded Knee: An Indian History of the American West.* New York: Henry Holt, 2001.

Brown, Larry K. *Coyotes and Canaries: Characters Who Made the West Wild . . . and Wonderful!* Glendo, WY: High Plains Press, 2002.

Buel, J. W. *Heroes of the Plains.* Philadelphia: Historical Publishing, 1881.

Burt, Nathaniel. *Compass American Guides: Wyoming.* 3rd ed. New York: Compass American Guides, 1998.

Canary, Martha. *Life and Adventures of Calamity Jane by Herself.* Fairfield, WA: Ye Galleon Press, 1979.

Carroll, John M., ed. *The Gibson-Edgerly Narrative.* Byron, TX: Private printing, 1977.

Cody, William F. *Buffalo Bill's Life Story: An Autobiography.* New York: Cosmopolitan Book Corporation, 1920.

———. *The Life of Hon. William F. Cody, Known as Buffalo Bill, the Famous Hunter, Scout and Guide: An Autobiography.* Hartford, CT: F. E. Bliss, 1879.

Connell, Evan S. *Son of the Morning Star: Custer and the Little Bighorn.* New York: Harper and Row, 1984.

Custer, Elizabeth B. *Following the Guidon.* Norman: University of Oklahoma Press, 1966.

David, Robert B. *Malcolm Campbell, Sheriff.* Casper, WY: Wyomingana, 1932.

Davis, John W. *Wyoming Range War: The Infamous Invasion of Johnson County.* Norman: University of Oklahoma Press, 2010.

Dawson, Charles. *Pioneer Tales of the Oregon Trail and of Jefferson County.* Topeka, KS: Topeka, Crane, 1912.

Donovan, James. *A Terrible Glory: Custer and the Little Bighorn—the Last Great Battle of the American West.* New York: Back Bay Books, 2008.

DuFran, Dora [d'Dée, pseud.]. *Low Down on Calamity Jane.* Rapid City, SD: N.p., 1932.

Dugan, Mark. *Tales Never Told around the Campfire: True Stories of the American Frontier.* Athens: Swallow Press/Ohio University Press, 1992.

Edward Clown Family, as told to William B. Matson. *Crazy Horse: The Warrior's Life and Legacy.* Layton, UT: Gibbs Smith, 2016.

Etulain, Richard W. *Calamity Jane: A Reader's Guide.* Norman: University of Oklahoma Press, 2015.

Friesen, Steve. *Buffalo Bill: Scout, Showman, Visionary.* Golden, CO: Fulcrum, 2010.

Gardner, Mark Lee. *Shot All to Hell: Jesse James, the Northfield Raid, and the Wild West's Greatest Escape*. New York: HarperCollins, 2013.

———. *To Hell on a Fast Horse: Billy the Kid, Pat Garrett, and the Epic Chase to Justice in the Old West*. New York: HarperCollins, 2010.

Garrett, Pat. *The Authentic Life of Billy, the Kid*. Santa Fe: New Mexican Printing and Publishing, 1882.

Graham, W. A. *The Story of the Little Big Horn: Custer's Last Fight*. Harrisburg, PA: Stackpole, 1959.

Gray, John S. *Centennial Campaign: The Sioux War of 1876*. Norman: University of Oklahoma Press, 1988.

Hammer, Kenneth, ed. *Custer in '76: Walter Camp's Notes on the Custer Fight*. Norman: University of Oklahoma Press, 1990.

Hedren, Paul L. *After Custer: Loss and Transformation in Sioux Country*. Norman: University of Oklahoma Press, 2011.

———. *First Scalp for Custer: The Skirmish at Warbonnet Creek, Nebraska, July 17, 1876*. Lincoln: Nebraska State Historical Society, 2005.

Hobsbawm, Eric J. *Primitive Rebels: Studies in Archaic Forms of Social Movement in the 19th and 20th Centuries*. New York: W. W. Norton, 1959.

Hughes, Richard B. *Pioneer Years in the Black Hills*. Rapid City, SD: Dakota Alpha Press, 2002.

Hutton, Paul Andrew. *The Apache Wars: The Hunt for Geronimo, the Apache Kid, and the Captive Boy Who Started the Longest War in American History*. New York: Broadway Books, 2016.

———, ed. *The Custer Reader*. Lincoln: University of Nebraska Press, 1992.

Jameson, W. C. *Billy the Kid: Beyond the Grave*. Lanham, MD: Taylor Trade, 2005.

Lake, Stuart N. *Wyatt Earp: Frontier Marshal*. Boston: Houghton Mifflin, 1931.

Lubet, Steven. *Murder in Tombstone: The Forgotten Trial of Wyatt Earp*. New Haven, CT: Yale University Press, 2004.

Maguire, Horatio. *Black Hills Wonderland*. Chicago: Donnelley, Lloyd, 1877.

Majors, Alexander. *Seventy Years on the Frontier*. Minneapolis: Ross and Haines, 1965.

Marshall, Joseph M., III. *The Journey of Crazy Horse: A Lakota History*. New York: Penguin Books, 2004.

McChristian, Douglas C. *Fort Laramie: Military Bastion of the High Plains*. Norman, OK: Arthur H. Clark, 2008.

McLaird, James D. *Calamity Jane: The Woman and the Legend*. Norman: University of Oklahoma Press, 2005.

———. *Wild Bill Hickok and Calamity Jane: Deadwood Legends*. Pierre: South Dakota State Historical Society Press, 2008.

Miles, Nelson A. *Personal Recollections and Observations of General Nelson A. Miles*. Chicago: Werner, 1896.

Moulton, Candy. *Valentine T. McGillycuddy: Army Surgeon, Agent to the Sioux*. Western Frontiersmen. Norman, OK: Arthur H. Clark, 2011.

Newark, Peter. *The Illustrated Encyclopedia of the Old West*. London: Brockhampton Press, 1998.

Nichols, Ronald Hamilton. *In Custer's Shadow: Major Marcus Reno.* Norman: University of Oklahoma Press, 1999.

Penrose, Charles B. *The Rustler Business.* Douglas, WY: Douglas Budget, 1959.

Powers, Thomas. *The Killing of Crazy Horse.* New York: Alfred A. Knopf, 2010.

Rezatto, Helen. *Mount Moriah: The Story of Deadwood's Boot Hill.* Rapid City, SD: Fenwyn Press, 1989.

Roberts, David. *Once They Moved Like the Wind: Cochise, Geronimo and the Apache Wars.* New York: Simon and Schuster, 1993.

Roberts, Richard A. *Reminiscences of General Custer: Custer's Last Battle.* Monroe, MI: Monroe County Library, 1978.

Rosa, Joseph G. *They Called Him Wild Bill: The Life and Adventures of James Butler Hickok.* Norman: University of Oklahoma Press, 1974.

———. *Wild Bill Hickok, Gunfighter: An Account of Hickok's Gunfights.* Norman: University of Oklahoma Press, 2003.

———. *Wild Bill Hickok: The Man and His Myth.* Lawrence: University Press of Kansas, 1996.

Russell, Don. *The Lives and Legends of Buffalo Bill.* Norman: University of Oklahoma Press, 1972.

Sandoz, Mari. *Crazy Horse: The Strange Man of the Oglalas.* 50th anniversary ed. Lincoln: University of Nebraska Press, 1961.

Silva, Lee A., and Silva, Susan Leiser. *Wyatt Earp: A Biography of the Legend.* Vol. 2, pt. 1, *Tombstone Before the Earps.* Santa Ana, CA: Graphic Publishers, 2010.

Slotkin, Richard. *Gunfighter Nation: The Myth of the Frontier in Twentieth-Century America.* Norman: University of Oklahoma Press, 1998.

Smith, Helena Huntington. *The War on Powder River.* New York: McGraw-Hill, 1966.

Spring, Agnes Wright. *The Cheyenne and Black Hills Stage and Express Routes.* Lincoln: University of Nebraska Press, 1967.

Stiles, T. J. *Custer's Trials: A Life on the Frontier of a New America.* New York: Alfred A. Knopf, 2015.

———. *Jesse James: Last Rebel of the Civil War.* New York: Vintage Books, 2003.

Stillman, Deanne. *Blood Brothers: The Story of the Strange Friendship between Sitting Bull and Buffalo Bill.* New York: Simon and Schuster, 2017.

Sweeney, Edwin R. *Cochise: Chiricahua Apache Chief.* Norman: University of Oklahoma Press, 1991.

———. *From Cochise to Geronimo: The Chiricahua Apaches, 1874–1889.* Norman: University of Oklahoma Press, 2010.

Tefertiller, Casey. *Wyatt Earp: The Life Behind the Legend.* New York: John Wiley, 1997.

Terry, Alfred H. *The Field Diary of General Alfred H. Terry: The Yellowstone Expedition—1876,* 2nd ed. Bellevue, NE: Old Army Press, 1970.

Trachtman, Paul. *The Gunfighters.* Old West. Alexandria, VA: Time-Life Books, 1974.

Trefousse, Hans Louis. *Ben Butler: The South Called Him Beast!* New York: Twayne, 1957.

Treuer, Anton. *The Indian Wars: Battles, Bloodshed, and the Fight for Freedom on the American Frontier.* Washington, DC: National Geographic Partners, 2016.

Turner, Alford E. *The O.K. Corral Inquest*. College Station, TX: Creative Publishing, 1981.

Tuska, Jon. *Billy the Kid: A Handbook*. Lincoln: University of Nebraska Press, 1983.

Utley, Robert M. *Billy the Kid: A Short and Violent Life*. Lincoln: University of Nebraska Press, 1989.

———. *Cavalier in Buckskin: George Armstrong Custer and the Western Military Frontier*. Rev. ed. Norman: University of Oklahoma Press, 2001.

———. *Geronimo*. New Haven, CT: Yale University Press, 2012.

Walker, Dale L. *Legends and Lies: Great Mysteries of the American West*. New York: Tom Doherty, 1997.

Warren, Louis S. *Buffalo Bill's America: William Cody and the Wild West Show*. New York: Alfred A. Knopf, 2005.

Wert, Jeffry D. *Custer: The Controversial Life of George Armstrong Custer*. New York: Touchstone, 1996.

Whittaker, Fredrick. *A Popular Life of Gen. George A. Custer*. New York: Sheldon, 1876.

Wilson, R. L. *Buffalo Bill's Wild West: An American Legend*. New York: Random House, 1998.

Wilstach, Frank J. *Wild Bill Hickok: The Prince of Pistoleers*. New York: Doubleday, Page, 1926.

Yeatman, Ted P. *Frank and Jesse James: The Story Behind the Legend*. Naperville, IL: Cumberland House, 2000.

Young, Harry. *Hard Knocks: A Life of the Vanishing West*. Portland, OR: J. K. Gill, 1915.

Younger, Thomas Coleman. *The Story of Cole Younger, by Himself*. Saint Paul: Minnesota Historical Society, 2000.

Periodicals

Boardman, Mark. "Wave of Violence: The Lynching of Tom Waggoner Marked the Start of the Johnson County War." *True West*, June 2016, 12.

Cutsforth, Kellen. "Evelyn Booth Took a Shot at Fame as a Partner of Buffalo Bill's Wild West: But Cody's English Benefactor Is Largely Forgotten Today." *Wild West* 26 (2014): 28–29.

Friesen, Steve. "The Man Behind the Legend." *American Cowboy*, collector's ed., 2012/2013, 48–55.

Lee, Jesse M. "The Capture and Death of an Indian Chieftain." *Journal of the Military Service Institution of the United States*, May–June 1914, 324–40.

McCanles, William Monroe. "The Only Living Eye Witness." *Nebraska Historical Magazine* 10, no. 2 (April–June 1927): 47–50.

The Northfield Bank Raid. Pamphlet. Northfield, MN: Northfield News, 2008. Reprinted from the *Northfield News*, 10th ed., August 27, September 3, 10, and 17, 1926.

Rocky Mountain News. "Governor Mabry Pins Imposter Tag on 'Billy the Kid.'" November 30, 1950.

Stone, A. C., J. E. Starrs, and M. Stoneking. "Mitochondrial DNA Analysis of the Presumptive Remains of Jesse James." *Journal of Forensic Sciences* 46, no. 1 (2001): 173–76.

Trimble, Marshall. "What Was Doc Holliday's Weapon of Choice? And How Authentic Is the Crossdraw Rig Worn by Val Kilmer While Portraying the Doc in 1993's *Tombstone*?" *True West*, December 2, 2006.

INTERNET RESOURCES

Adams, Guy. "The Big Question: Who Was Geronimo, and Why Is There Controversy over His Remains?" *Independent*, June 22, 2009. Accessed January 23, 2017. www .independent.co.uk/news/world/americas/the-big-question-who-was-geronimo -and-why-is-there-controversy-over-his-remains-1714167.html.

Bray, Kingsley M. "Crazy Horse Genealogy." American-Tribes.com. Accessed May 17, 2017. www.american-tribes.com/Lakota/BIO/CrazyHorse.htm.

Broome, Jeff. "Death at Summit Springs: Susanna Alderdice and the Cheyennes." HistoryNet.com. Accessed March 13, 2017. www.historynet.com/death-at -summit-springs-susanna-alderdice-and-the-cheyennes.htm.

Coffman, Keith. "Rare Billy the Kid Photograph Sold for $2.3 Million." Reuters, June 27, 2011. Accessed April 15, 2017. www.reuters.com/article/us-auction-billykid -photo-idUSTRE75O1HX20110627.

Fairbury.com. "Rock Creek Station State Historical Park." Accessed May 12, 2017. www.fairbury.com/pages/history/rock_creek.html.

Hutton, Paul Andrew. "Was Geronimo a Terrorist? Tracing America's View of the Apache Warrior from Bloodthirsty Terrorist to Patriot Chief." *True West*, July 28, 2011. Accessed January 23, 2017. https://truewestmagazine.com/was-geronimo-a -terrorist/.

Jones, William B., Jr. "Introduction: Buffalo Bill Illustrated." In *Classics Illustrated: A Cultural History*. Jefferson, NC: McFarland, 2011. Google Books. Accessed March 16, 2017. https://books.google.com/books?id=1SjtAQAAQBAJ&pg=PT50&lpg =PT50&dq=sitting+bull+respected+Buffalo+Bill+only+white+man&source =bl&ots=syW-kIlpPA&sig=tCQOhk4n8zpibS2wtDvlj-EJdfQ&hl=en&sa=X &ved=0ahUKEwjd5-6ZxtzSAhVI-2MKHc2vCH8Q6AEIUTAO#v=onepage &q=sitting%20bull%20respected%20Buffalo%20Bill%20only%20white%20man &f=false.

Lannon, Albert Vetere. "134 Years Later—the Gunfight at the O.K. Corral." *Desert Times*, October 7, 2015. Accessed January 23, 2017. www.tucsonlocalmedia.com/ deserttimes/article_1d9faaec-6d11-11e5-943f-e7a9fb91172a.html.

Maxfield, Max. *Constitution of the State of Wyoming*. November 12, 2008. Wyoming Secretary of State website. Accessed April 5, 2017. https://soswy.state.wy.us/Forms/ Publications/09WYConstitution.pdf.

Nightengale, Robert. "Battle of Little Bighorn Coverup." HistoryNet.com. Accessed August 22, 2017. www.historynet.com/battle-of-little-bighorn.

Tefertiller, Casey, and Jeff Morey. "O.K. Corral: A Gunfight Shrouded in Mystery." HistoryNet.com. Accessed January 30, 2017. www.historynet.com/ok-corral.

Thayer, Bill. "George A. Custer." Bill Thayer's website. Accessed April 29, 2017. http://penelope.uchicago.edu/Thayer/E/Gazetteer/Places/America/United_States/Army/USMA/Cullums_Register/1966*.html.

Wyoming Statutes. § 6-4-413 (2014). "Rustling; penalty." Justia. Accessed April 1, 2017. http://law.justia.com/codes/wyoming/2014/title-6/chapter-3/article-4/section-6-3-413.

Weiser, Kathy. "Old West Legends: John William Poe—Hunting Billy the Kid." Legends of America. Accessed April 15, 2017. www.legendsofamerica.com/law-johnpoe.html.

———. "Wyoming Legends: Johnson County War." Legends of America. Accessed March 27, 2017. www.legendsofamerica.com/wy-johnsoncountywar.html.

Wikipedia. "American Exhibition." Wikipedia. Accessed March 14, 2107. https://en.wikipedia.org/wiki/American_Exhibition#cite_note-considered-4.

———. "Johnson County War." Accessed March 28, 2017. https://en.wikipedia.org/wiki/Johnson_County_War.

Wyoming Stock Growers Association. "Wyoming Stock Growers Association: Guardians of Wyoming's Cow Country Since 1872." 2017. Wyoming Stock Growers Association website. Accessed April 4, 2017. www.wysga.org/aboutwsga.aspx.

INDEX

ABOUT THE AUTHORS

Bill Markley is a member of Western Writers of America (WWA) and a staff writer for WWA's *Roundup* magazine. He has written three non-fiction books: *Dakota Epic: Experiences of a Reenactor during the Filming of* Dances with Wolves; *Up the Missouri River with Lewis and Clark*; and *American Pilgrim: A Post–September 11th Bus Trip and Other Tales of the Road*. He writes for *True West, Wild West*, and *South Dakota* magazines. His fourth book, *Deadwood Dead Men*, is Bill's first historical novel. Western Fictioneers selected *Deadwood Dead Men* as a finalist for its 2014 Peacemaker Award in the category Best First Western Novel. Bill also wrote the "Military Establishment" chapter and thirty entries for the *Encyclopedia of Western Expansion* (2011). Bill manages WWA's Facebook page as well as Old West and American History Facebook pages. He was a member of Toastmasters International for twenty years. He earned a bachelor's degree in biology and a master's degree in environmental sciences and engineering at Virginia Tech, worked on two Antarctic field teams, and worked for forty years with the South Dakota Department of Environment and Natural Resources. Raised on a farm near Valley Forge, Pennsylvania, Bill has always loved history. He reenacts Civil War infantry and frontier cavalry and has participated in the films *Dances with Wolves, Son of the Morning Star, Far and Away, Gettysburg*, and *Crazy Horse*. Bill and his wife, Liz, live in Pierre, South Dakota, where they have raised two children, now grown.

Kellen Cutsforth is the author of *Buffalo Bill, Boozers, Brothels and Bare Knuckle Brawlers: An Englishman's Journal of Adventure in America* (2015) and *Buffalo Bill's Wild West Coloring Book* (2017), and he has also provided ghostwriting services for multiple books and projects. Kellen has published more than thirty articles featured in such publications as *Wild West*, *True West*, WWA's *Roundup* magazine, and the Denver Posse of Westerners *Roundup* periodical. Kellen is an active member of WWA and runs its Twitter account. He is also a contributor to the *Western History* blog for the Denver Public Library. His blogs have been featured in *Archives Open* national online periodical. Kellen is a veteran speaker and presenter and has made multiple presentations for numerous history groups, libraries, and genealogical organizations. Kellen also served as a past president of the Denver Posse of Westerners.